Psychology and Pop Culture

Psychology and Pop Culture

An Empirical Adventure

by
Keith W. Beard, April Fugett,
and Britani Black

LEXINGTON BOOKS
Lanham • Boulder • New York • London

Published by Lexington Books
An imprint of The Rowman & Littlefield Publishing Group, Inc.
4501 Forbes Boulevard, Suite 200, Lanham, Maryland 20706
www.rowman.com

6 Tinworth Street, London SE11 5AL, United Kingdom

British Library Cataloguing in Publication Information Available

Library of Congress Cataloging-in-Publication Data

Library of Congress Control Number: 2020952328
ISBN: 9781793624680 (cloth)
ISBN: 9781793624703 (pbk)
ISBN: 9781793624697 (electronic)

Contents

Preface

A Memoir of a Con Family

A little over eight years ago, Dr. Keith Beard and Dr. April Fugett were having a conversation about research and teaching. Dr. Fugett had just created a psychology of pop culture course for our department and had proposed her first honors seminar, and Dr. Beard was teaching courses about comic books and psychology and paranormal psychology. These courses, in multiple iterations and across multiple terms, were some of the most fun and most popular courses that we taught. The only problem was that we both kept running into the same issue . . . a veritable lack of research and data analysis on the phenomenon that we were interested in. We decided that the best way to tackle this issue was to jump headfirst into research.

Dr. Fugett's master's degree is a general psychology M.A., and her Ph.D. is in cognitive psychology. Her interests are primarily in language, memory, research methodology, and statistical analyses. She has taught a wide array of courses for every departmental program at our university, from Introduction to Psychology for our Freshmen to Advanced Quantitative Analysis for fourth-year doctoral students. She brings all these areas of expertise and experience into our research.

Dr. Beard's master's degree is in clinical psychology, and his Psy.D. degree is in clinical psychology. Beyond his academic work, he has worked in university counseling centers, community mental health centers, and currently has a small private practice. His interests are primarily in abnormal psychology, personality, sexuality studies, and Internet addiction. Dr. Beard has also taught a wide array of courses (Introductory Psychology, Paranormal Phenomena, Abnormal Psychology, Personality, and Human Sexuality) and incorporates those into our projects.

We started with our most basic question: "How does personality influence our choices in the superheroes that we choose to love and hate?" As the two of us talked in the hallways and stole time in each other's office to discuss Institutional Review Board (IRB) paperwork and personality measures and superheroes, we discovered that some of our students were just as interested in these topics as we were. We very quickly found that we had a lab and two students, in particular, who were interested in many of the same things we were. We put them both to work, made no promises, and the contents of this book were born. Eighteen current and completed studies, following the progression of our thought process as we designed and tested each one. Each study is housed firmly within the field of psychology, is IRB vetted and approved, and has been designed and analyzed to answer questions from across many areas of our expertise. Each conclusion is grounded in its unique dataset, and these 18 completed studies form the basis for the ongoing work in our lab. Parts and pieces of many of these studies have been presented at conferences and comic conventions across the country, but the culmination of the complete analysis have not been included until now.

Along the way, our students became our colleagues, and Dr. Britani Black has moved from being a research assistant in her first year to first author and co-author on several of the projects. Dr. Black has also taught a wide array of courses, including Internet Famous: Language, Health, and Psychology in the Age of the New Celebrity and The Heroes and Villains of Healthcare, and has clinical expertise in interpersonal theories, substance use, and the young adult population that she now uses to inform our projects.

We also want to take the time to thank our graduate students who worked hard with us on our various projects discussed in this book. While they did not work directly on this text, they did help with parts of various studies, and we would like to acknowledge this. Even though they are all now professionals, or on the path to being one, they will always be our "con kids." They include:

Josh Carter	Jacob Mills
Carrie Dean	Casey Collins
Krista Harris	Kasey Kessler
Jake Bass	Jason Duncan
and Elijah Wise	

If you are an academic reading this book, you will see that we have held each study to the rigor expected for any peer-reviewed publication or journal article. If you are a psychologist, you will see us use the terms of our profession. If you are an undergraduate student reading this book, you will get a feel for introductory level psychology in the context of some of your favorite heroes and villains from across a wide array of pop culture examples and genres. If you are a member of the lay audience, you will find that our experiences in presenting to lay audiences at various comic conventions have given us a certain voice. It is with this unique voice that you can expect us to write.

We will discuss the Dark Triad of personality, Bonferroni corrections, and how very cool it is to be asked about personality preferences by someone in full Deadpool cosplay. You will find an index and citations where appropriate, for the discerning audience. We will also occasionally throw in how we've incorporated findings into other areas of our careers, whether those are in therapy sessions or in the classroom. Most of all, we hope you have as much fun reading this book, and gain as much knowledge, as we did putting it all together. Oh, and one last thing, this is your only potential spoiler alert. We are assuming that by the time this book hits the shelves, our readers have had plenty of time to watch, read, or listen to anything about any of the things we reference, including their endings. You've been warned.

Chapter One

Personality, Superheroes, Science Fiction, Fantasy, and Psychology

As we said in the preface, the reader can expect the scientific approach and academic style in this text, but you will also get just as much of our individual preferences and disagreements. If you are an academic reading this peer-reviewed book, you will find each study is held to the rigor expected for any peer-reviewed publication or journal article with just a touch more enthusiasm in the discussion than is the norm. If you are a psychologist, you will notice the use of terms of our profession. If you are an undergraduate, you will be exposed to concepts related to introductory level psychology in the context of some of your favorite pop culture examples and genres. If you are a member of the lay audience, you will find that our experiences in presenting at various comic conventions have given us a certain voice in how we discuss, collaborate on, and debate our results. You can expect to read this text with this unique voice of both scholarship and enthusiasm.

All three of us love popular culture, from the superheroes to the sweeping fantasies to quirky sitcoms to everything in between. We are fans. Keith is our DC Universe person. He can go on and on about every character and every power. And don't get him started on Superman breaking Zod's neck in the *Man of Steel* film (Peters, Phillips, Tull, and Snyder, 2013)! April is our horror fan. She knows every vampire reference there is, from the good (*Salem's Lot* . . . really all things Stephen King) to the bad (yes, we will be talking about *Twilight* in a bit). Britani has been tasked with creating our characters lists for years now and is a little all over the place. She would jokingly say she is a SuperWhoLock fan because she can never pick just one favorite. But really, we can all talk a little bit about everything.

At the end of the day, that is the beauty of popular culture. It really is a little of everything and encompasses something for everyone. The term itself has been in use since the 1950s and has grown to encompass more and

more as media and technology have grown. It covers everything from literature, music, television, and movies to the authors and artists responsible for
bringing the characters, lyrics, and stories to life (Danesi, 2012). There is
little doubt that pop culture has taken on a life of its own and factors into the
everyday lives of many of us. We have watercooler talks over cliffhangers
and disappointing finales. We take a break from the chaos of work to see the
newest action flick. Or we tune into a YouTube video on our lunch hour to
distract ourselves and take a break. Whatever aspect of pop culture that you
have some interest in, you can find it with merchandise, fanfiction, streaming services, books, movies, televisions shows—everywhere. Pop culture
as a concept has only grown in popularity. Yet, there are many questions
behind why an individual consumes, follows, and likes certain aspects of
popular culture over others. In essence, this has been something we have
spent nearly a decade trying to understand. We study what we know; so, in
many ways, we are trying to research ourselves and the millions of other
pop culture fans out there.

Before we get into the research and the results of our studies, you will need
to have a basis for the theories behind our research. While this isn't always
the "fun stuff" that you want to read about, it is important to understand so
you have a better idea of why and how we studied this topic. We are all educators after all, so we want to start with the science. With our initial study that
started this journey, we set out to see how a person's personality can be used
to predict favorite characters.

Therefore, we first need to understand what personality is. Personality is
based on the Latin word, *persona*, which refers to the mask used by actors
in a play. The word "personality" came to refer to the outward appearance;
the public face that we display to those around us. We refer to more than
the visible aspects of ourselves that others see and the superficial qualities.
The word also encompasses social, emotional, and internal qualities. It may
include enduring or lasting qualities and/or unique and special qualities that
distinguish us from others. One psychologist (Adams, 1954) suggested that
we define personality as—I—because when you say "I" you are in effect
summing up everything about yourself. Psychologists do not agree on a single definition of "personality," but here is one that we use for you to have as
a basis: *Personality—the unique and relatively stable and enduring internal
and external characteristics, including thoughts, feelings and actions, that
influence behavior and may change in response to different situations.*

Psychologists devote a lot of time developing theories to try and explain
what your personality is and how your personality developed. Pearce (2003)
discusses one of the first personality theories that was derived from Freud.
In essence, Freud's theory is a developmental theory since it involves the

idea that human development is governed by a sequence of stages that occurred beginning at birth and throughout childhood and into adulthood. He felt that a person's development and past/childhood experiences influenced the person's personality. Freud proposed five psychosexual stages of development with specific tasks or experiences that needed to occur for a healthy and happy personality. These stages include: 1) Oral; 2) Anal; 3) Phallic; 4) Latency; and 5) Genital. If normal development is blocked or if a particular task that needs to be accomplished during a stage does not get resolved then a fixation occurs in that stage and results in a problem with one's personality, interpersonal style, and relationships. Likewise, Freud felt that there were unconscious forces that impact our actions, behaviors, likes, dislikes, and so on. These unconscious forces include the Id, Ego, and Superego. When there is conflict between these unconscious forces then there are psychological problems that develop as well as problematic personality styles.

Many felt that Freud's theory, although popular in its time, did not fully explain how personality develops. Since his initial theories, psychologists have moved on to note theories rooted in biology, behavior, and more. From a biological standpoint, John, Robins, and Pervin (2008) describe how personality is the product of hereditary factors that are the result of the genetic makeup that a person receives from the father and mother. For example, have you ever been told that you are stubborn like your father or outspoken like your mother? Whether the person saying that about you realizes it or not, that person is using the biological theory to explain your personality. An additional aspect of the biological theory has to do with biochemistry, which involves hormones and neurotransmitters within the body. These chemicals have been found to influence mood, behavior, and thoughts.

Finally, the biological theory would suggest that we are born with a particular temperament. For example, one mother may say that she has a "fussy" baby, suggesting that the child is often upset or not easily soothed. Another mother may say that her child is an "easy" baby indicating that the child is typically happy, calm, and tolerates frustration. The biological theory would suggest that this temperament is the basis of our personality as we grow and progress into childhood, adolescence, and adulthood. Evolution, a branch of the biological theory, suggests that there are personality traits such as being cooperative and helpful that assist to ensure the survival of the species. Therefore, these personality aspects become more prominent in a person.

Burger (2017) states that from a behavioral standpoint, personality is shaped by learning. Classical conditioning, operant conditioning, and modeling are common ways that the theories from the behavioral approach explain how learning occurs. For example, a person may have that one food that she ate and then for whatever reason, she became sick and now associates that food with being sick. Now that person may be described as a "picky eater" because of the association that has been made between a once neutral food and the resulting illness. Alternatively, a person may be reinforced or punished for behaving or demonstrating certain personality styles. This would influence the continuation or extinction of that personality style in order to continue to gain more positive results or minimize negative consequences. Additionally, we can observe those around us and learn vicariously from their experiences. For example, a child may see his mother being anxious and therefore begins to view the world as a place to be scared of and develop an anxious personality style.

These are only a few of the theories that have been proposed to explain personality development and other psychological aspects of a person. Just like a single definition for "personality" cannot be agreed upon, the debate over the best or most appropriate theory to explain personality is an ongoing argument among psychologists. All these theories have merit and varying levels of research behind them, and any one of them could have been applied to the research we will discuss in this book. However, the approach that we used to study personality is called the trait approach due to reasons we will outline in just a moment. Before we get into that, let's first define a trait. A "trait" is an aspect of personality used to categorize people according to the degree to which they have, show, or manifest a particular characteristic.

There are two assumptions that "trait" psychologists make. The first is that personality characteristics are relatively stable over time. For example, you do not typically have high self-esteem one day and low self-esteem another day. Although we do have our ups and downs, trait psychologists maintain that over a long period of time a relatively stable level of self-esteem can be identified and used to predict behavior. The second assumption is that personality characteristics are stable across situations. For example, if you hold the trait of being "hot headed" then you lose your temper easily at a football game, at school, at your spouse, or at others.

In contrast to traits, there are states. A "state" is a temporary and fleeting aspect of personality that varies based on the situation, condition, or perceptions that the person is having at the time. For example, you are under a great deal of stress and someone irritates you by asking you numerous, unimportant, silly questions. You become annoyed. However, this isn't a typical or consistent aspect of your personality but is only triggered because of this situation.

According to the trait theory, almost any personality characteristic can be illustrated on the trait continuum. If we studied a large number of people, we would more than likely find that there was a normal distribution or "bell-shaped curve" with few people at the extremely high end of having a particular trait; a few people at the extremely low end of having the same trait; and the majority of people somewhere in the middle.

Bell-Shaped Curve

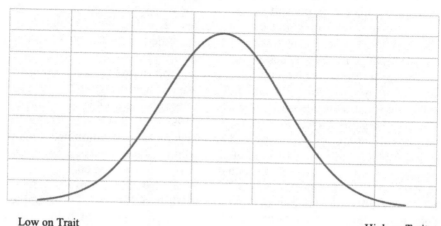

Low on Trait

High on Trait

Figure 1.1.   Trait Continuum Chart.
Created by the authors.

So, we could take various traits, and place them on the continuum with a personality aspect such as sadness on one end of the continuum and happiness on the other end. We would assume that there are few people who are happy a large portion of the time; few people who sad a large portion of the time; and the majority of people having a balance between being happy and sad. The same could be done with other traits such as introverted versus extraverted or anxious versus fearless or optimistic versus pessimistic. When we look at traits, we are most interested in how people who score on a certain segment of the continuum *typically* behave as opposed to how they behave in a certain situation. This allows for us to get a better sense of their stable personality aspects.

Trait psychologists are also more interested in describing personality and predicting behavior rather than explaining why people behave the way they do. Why a personality aspect may or may not have developed is not the focus, and this theory does not really address personality change, unlike some of the other personality theories. As a result, this theory is more likely to be used by researchers than therapists. There are several advantages to using the trait theory for research. First, with this theory, it is easy to make comparisons across people. We can simply place the person on the continuum and compare where that person is to other people. Second, since this theory is often used by researchers, it is, obviously, highly researched. Finally, this approach to studying personality has several practical applications. For example, it is easy to use in mental health settings, employment, and education.

There are also some criticisms of the trait approach. First, as mentioned previously, this theory doesn't explain how or why traits develop. Secondly, since having a particular trait can sometimes be problematic, it doesn't go into how to help people who score in the extreme ranges (high or low) on a trait. Finally, there is a lack of agreement on what the traits are and the number of traits someone could possess or exhibit. Some theorists say there are too many categories. For example, Eysenck (Goldberg and Rosolack, 1994) said that there are only three main traits (i.e., neuroticism—extraversion/introversion—psychoticism). Digman (1997) said that there were really only two super factors (i.e., alpha and beta), which actually combined several traits. Alpha is said to include emotional stability, agreeableness, conscientiousness, while beta is said to include extraversion and openness to new experience. Additionally, there is debate about what to call various traits or how to describe the components that might fall into that trait. For example, does being "brave" include "fearless?" One might argue that being brave includes fear but still engaging in the brave behavior despite having that fear. Another might argue that "courageous" is a better name for the trait and that both "brave" and "fearless" fall under this trait. Hopefully you are starting to see why psychologists have such a difficult time agreeing on definitions of personality and what makes up our personality.

One of the trait approach theories is the Big Five Personality Factors. This theory, described by John and Srivastava (1999) contains five personality dimensions:

1. Neuroticism (more commonly referred to now as emotional stability)—this dimension examines personal and emotional adjustment. On one end of the continuum, you are easily upset, insecure, worry, and have self-pity. On the other end of the continuum, you would not be easily bothered by things, you would be cheerful and confident.
2. Extraversion—this dimension explores how introverted/extraverted you are. On one end of the continuum, you are energetic, outgoing, optimistic, friendly, and assertive. On the other end of the continuum, you are withdrawn, quiet, shy, and reserved.
3. Openness—this dimension examines how open to experiences a person is. On one end of the continuum, you are open to new experiences, imaginative, like variety, and independent. On the other end of the continuum, you are closed to new experiences, dull, ordinary, needy, and boring.
4. Agreeableness—this dimension explores how compassionate and cooperative you are. On one end of the continuum, you are helpful, trusting, and sympathetic. On the other end of the continuum, you are uncooperative, antagonistic, negative, and callous.

5. Conscientiousness—this dimension explores how controlled or self-disciplined you are. On one end of the continuum, you are well organized, careful, self-controlled, determined. On the other end of the continuum, you are unstructured, impulsive, careless, and indecisive.

Beyond generating theories, psychologists have looked at how to evaluate or assess your personality. There are multiple ways to measure the Big Five personality dimension. One way is a self-report survey called the Big Five Inventory (John and Srivastava, 1999). The Big Five Inventory (BFI) has allowed researchers to measure how an individual rates on the Big Five traits (openness, conscientiousness, extraversion, agreeableness, neuroticism/emotional stability) via a self-report measure (John and Srivastava, 1999). The number of items has been deliberated as researchers have debated what questions on the instrument best reflect the personality traits themselves. The NEO was once considered the standard measure for the Big Five but was later thought of as too long and cumbersome to administer when conducting research such as this (Costa and McCrae, 1985; Rammstedt and John, 2007). However, the 44 item BFI has proven reliable (average alpha reliability > .80) and useful in a variety of research situations (John and Srivastava, 1999), including research related to popular culture and personality traits (Kraaykamp and van Eijck, 2005). The BFI provides a measure that not only gives valid information for researchers but is also user friendly for participants due to the nature of the items. Each of the 44 statements are short in nature and allow for an easier and efficient way to measure all five of the personality traits in the Big Five theory (John and Srivastava, 1999). As you will see in all of our chapters, we have chosen to use the BFI as our measure of choice.

Now that we have talked about some basic terms and measures of personality, we want to discuss our initial study. We want to emphasize that our studies (all of them . . . even the ones not represented in this text) have been thoroughly vetted by our Office of Research Integrity (ORI), commonly referred to as the Institutional Review Board (IRB). Only after careful evaluation by our ORI are our studies conducted via the measures outlined in the approved protocol.

When it came time to gather data, we constructed a survey comprised of four parts. Participants initially gave consent to the study and the conditions. They then completed our demographic questions and then participants encountered questions related to the final two components, personality traits with the BFI and popular culture character preference.

The demographic questions covered basic information about participants, such as gender identification, age, sexual orientation, and education. We used this to further understand what factors relate to certain personality traits as well as character preference. Demographics have been an ever-evolving component of our survey. In fact, almost every single study in this book has required a bit of a tweak, here or there. We have created appendix A to address our demographics, past and present. While we reference it here, the information really applies to each chapter in the book. Whenever we discuss our demographics (or report them in our results section), please feel free to reference appendix A.

In addition to the demographics, we created a list of popular culture characters. The list includes a mix of heroes, villains, and famous characters. Science fiction, fantasy, and popular media (television, film, literature, and comic books) from the zeitgeist were examined for characters for a full list. This is one of the components of the study that is truly unique to us. The list spans characters far and wide across each of a variety of nerddoms. Additionally, we utilized information gathered from fan culture, such as Tumblr, Twitter, and fanfiction, to better understand which characters fit into each trope. As was the case with our demographics, these characters have grown to take on a life of their own. They also seem to apply to every single chapter in this book (especially chapter 10, but that involves spoiler alerts). Please see appendix B for a SAMPLE of our characters and a brief discussion on why we are not sharing our full list (and that is only partially because that list—or those lists—would take up a substantial portion of this book). If you have more questions than appendix B can resolve, feel free to find us on social media and reach out.

For the first study we conducted, we ultimately came up with a list of over 200 pop culture characters that were alphabetized to mix up various media venues and characters. We asked participants to rate how much they "like" the character (1 = Strongly dislike, while 5 = Strongly like), and then they were asked to rate them again based on how much they "identify" with the character (1 = Strongly do not identify, while 5 = Strongly identify). We thought it was particularly important to separate these out because whether you like or dislike a character can be very different from whether you identify with that character—or so we thought, as you will see from our results. This is the only study where we asked both questions, and it is one of only two studies that relied on the one to five scale. We realized early on that this limited scale did not give us enough "range" to tease apart differences. You will see this shift to a larger scale in later chapters. Additionally, because we were well aware our list was extensive and not everyone would know every character, participants could mark "does not know" the character, so that a lack of knowledge regarding a character did not influence the results.

We used three primary tools to collect this dataset and distribute our survey: Amazon's Mechanical Turk (MTurk), SONA, and Qualtrics. The specific function of Amazon's Mechanical Turk (MTurk, www.MTurk.com) system is to recruit participants for research. MTurk is viewed by social scientists as a newer resource that allows for the recruitment of a wide range of diverse participants. Additionally, MTurk users have been found to generate high-quality survey data (e.g., adequate internal consistency and test-retest reliability coefficients) for rewards as low as $0.02 (Buhrmester, Kwang, and Gosling, 2011). There has been some evidence that data collected via sources like MTurk have good generalizability and seem to be relatively representative of the population of interest (Gosling, Vazire, Srivastava, and John, 2004), at least more so than the usual convenience sampling that we often see on college campuses. Speaking of convenience sampling, we also used the SONA system. This program is utilized by the Marshall University Psychology Department to recruit participants for human subjects research. Undergraduate students at Marshall University who are enrolled in psychology courses can sign up to participate in research experiments and receive extra credit in their respective psychology course.

Finally, the dataset for this research project was generated using Qualtrics software (Version XM of Qualtrics, Copyright © 2018 Qualtrics, Qualtrics and all other Qualtrics product or service names are registered trademarks or trademarks of Qualtrics, Provo, UT, USA). Qualtrics (http://www.qualtrics.com) allows researchers to design and host surveys completely online. This software uses Security Sockets Layer protocol to securely collect and store data, allows for multiple question types (i.e., single and multiple response, response grids, numeric, and open-ended), and is compatible with MTurk and SPSS Inc. (and later by SPSS IBM Corp) statistical analysis software.

We do acknowledge, as with any research design, that there are some potential flaws in our research method. For example, with our characters, the list could be too broad, too narrow, or too long. Since we did have many listed characters, it is possible that participants could become fatigued, engage in random responses, or drop out of the study. In terms of the measures, some could argue that the BFI was not the best instrument to measure personality; however, we are happy with our previously discussed reasoning for using this instrument since it is an easily accessible and scorable measure.

Before we get into the juicy details and what everyone probably wants to know (i.e., did your favorite character top the list), we want to also acknowledge that not all these characters are as popular or well known today. For this reason, we have listed the pop culture source material for the characters the first time that they are mentioned in each chapter. We chose to go in this direction since we understand that not all will know ever character and that certain chapters may be read while others may be ignored based on the class, lecture, or other reason for buying this book. Hopefully you will get to read about your favorite characters and maybe discover some new ones that you might want to learn more about. Now . . . to the results.

Our most liked characters, in order, were Gandalf (*LOTR*), Batman (*DC Universe*), Iron Man (*Marvel Universe*), Aragorn (*LOTR*), Dean Winchester (*Supernatural*), Katniss Everdeen (*Hunger Games*), Spock (*Star Trek*), Chewbacca (*Star Wars*), Professor X (*Marvel Universe*), Legolas (*LOTR*), and Obi-Wan Kenobi (*Star Wars*). Of particular note (and a hint of chapters to come) was the fact that only a single female was in our top ten, and there was some serious representation for specific fandoms (*Lord of the Rings* and *Star Wars* spring to mind). Our least liked characters, in order, were President Snow (*Hunger Games*), Aro (*Twilight*), Bella Swan (*Twilight*), Victoria (*Twilight*), Cauis (*Twilight*), Jane (*Twilight*), Jar Jar Binks (*Star Wars*), The Governor (*The Walking Dead*), Edward Cullen (*Twilight*), and James (*Twilight*).

Some of these were true bad guys, the kind of villains we love to hate, and we expected them to be on our list (President Snow, The Governor, and poor Jar Jar Binks still makes almost every most hated list we have ever created). The really shocking thing, however, was the absolute hate for *Twilight*. Renesmee (*Twilight*) edged out Saruman (*LOTR*) by a significant margin to take spot 11. This intense dislike (or backlash) against *Twilight* held for several years. Interestingly, beginning with a 2019 dataset, we saw a new wave of backlash for a very unexpected franchise. As we have continued to examine characters over the last decade or so, we have seen many such shifts in the most and least liked characters. Likewise, we have seen some franchises and fandoms increase and decrease in popularity. So, we have adjusted our character list as our research has progressed. In some of our later chapters, you will see that we have some lists with well over 500 characters, and we've started to collect them separately to combat list fatigue. This will be discussed more in future chapters when we explain the results for different studies we have conducted.

When examining the BFI (John and Srivastava, 1999), we found some interesting results. All exploratory stepwise regression analyses were completed examining all eight sub-components of personality. As always, a Bonferroni correction was conducted to counter the number of analyses conducted and to protect our Type I error rate; the significance level has been lowered from $p < .05$ to $p < .005$ to determine significance. When people were asked to rate characters that they "like," there were certain characters that were associated with each of the five personality dimensions. Those who scored high on agreeableness (helpful, sympathetic) significantly like the following characters: Aragorn, Chewbacca, Green Lantern (*DC Universe*), Jabba the Hutt (*Star Wars*), Lando Calrissian (*Star Wars*), Luke Skywalker (*Star Wars*), Nightwing (*DC Universe*), and Princess Leia (*Star Wars*). There were no significant findings for characters when we looked at those who scored low on agreeableness (distrustful, antagonistic), but we did seem several of those who scored high on conscientiousness (disciplined, organized) and significantly liked Aslan (*Chronicles of Narnia*), Bella Swan (*Twilight*), Cinna (*Hunger Games*), John Winchester (*Supernatural*), Sam Winchester, Dean Winchester, Legolas, Han Solo, Hawkeye (*Marvel Universe*), and Haymitch (*Hunger Games*). In contrast, those who scored low on conscientiousness (careless, spontaneous) significantly liked the following characters: Boba Fett (*Star Wars*), Chewbacca, Jabba the Hutt, and Catwoman (*DC Universe*). It is interesting to note that most of these characters could be considered antiheroes. We will acknowledge that there are very different views of Jabba the Hutt, Chewbacca, and Boba Fett, but we should all be able to agree that they are all not all law-abiding citizens. The same can be said for Catwoman.

These were not the only interesting results that we found. Those who scored high on emotional stability/neuroticism (stressed, upset) were more apt to significantly like Alfred (*DC Universe*), Lando Calrissian (*Star Wars*), and Boba Fett; those who scored low on emotional stability/neuroticism (cheerful, calm) were more prone to significantly like Bella Swan, Edward Cullen, Jacob Black (*Twilight*), Buffy Summers (*Buffy the Vampire Slayer*), Peeta Mellark (*Hunger Games*), Thor (*Marvel Universe*), Lando Calrissian, Red Skull (*Marvel Universe*), and Captain Kirk (*Star Trek*). We are not sure what the driving force was for this burst of character liking. There is an easily discernable vampire theme or Young Adult fiction theme, but that does not account for Red Skull or Captain Kirk. It did elicit an important question though. Which Captain Kirk were we asking about? This is something we have since debated thoroughly and left largely up for interpretation by those taking the survey. With reboots, sequels, and adaptions increasing in popularity, we continue to monitor these trends and have been discussing further directions to this even as we write this chapter.

Back to the research at hand: in regard to personality, there were no statistically significant findings discovered for those who scored significantly high or low on openness and which characters they reportedly liked. The same can be said for those who scored significantly high or low on the extraversion/introversion scale and which characters they liked most.

When we examined which characters were most and least "identified" with, we found just a few subtle differences on our most and least identified-with characters. Our most identified-with characters in order were: Katniss Everdeen (*Hunger Games*), Kaylee Frye (*Firefly*), Sam Winchester, Hiro Nakamura (*Heroes*), Maggie Green (*The Walking Dead*), Samwise Gamgee (*LOTR*), Dean Winchester, Beast/Hank McCoy (*Marvel Universe*), Hurley Reyes (*Lost*), and Professor X; our least identified-with characters were

President Snow, Jabba the Hutt, Jar Jar Binks, and a slew of Twilight characters including Jane, Aro, James, Saruman, Victoria, Caius, Renesmee, and Edward Cullen. Yes, we know that Edward makes the 11 most hated instead of the 10, but we wanted to point out that it was not just the "bad guys" of Twilight not feeling the love . . . him . . . and poor Jar Jar Binks.

We do want to mention that when we compared "liked" characters with characters that participants "identified" with, there were not any major differences between the lists. So, we concluded that whether you like or identify with a character was probably tapping into the same concept. As a result, we stopped separating these lists into those two categories and just continued in our future research with looking at characters that were "liked."

The coolest results (yes, April insists on the word coolest) actually previews a couple of the other chapters in the book. We also examined how self-identified gender predicted how much we like specific characters. A total of 95 male identifying and 184 female identifying participants were used in the analysis. Males were more likely to "like" the following characters: Darth Vader, Chewbacca, Boba Fett, Mace Windu (*Star Wars*), Obi-Wan Kenobi, Padme Amidala (*Star Wars*), Jabba the Hutt, Bane (*DC Universe*), Batman, Joker (*DC Universe*), Flash (*DC Universe*), Green Lantern (*DC Universe*), Daredevil (*Marvel Universe*), Magneto (*Marvel Universe*), Professor X, Wolverine (*Marvel Universe*), Red Skull (*Marvel Universe*), Spider-Man (*Marvel Universe*), Warpath (*Marvel Universe*), Gandalf, Gimli, Gollum (*LOTR*), Green Goblin (*Marvel Universe*), Saruman (*LOTR*), Kahn (*Star Trek*), and Merle Dixon (*The Walking Dead*). Female identifying participants were more likely to like Aslan, Dean Winchester, Edward Cullen, Jacob Black, Effie Trinket (*The Hunger Games*), Peeta Mellark, and Jar Jar Binks. Three important notes here. First, male identifying and female identifying individuals like very different types of fandoms (Marvel and DC for males versus Young Adult fiction for females). Secondly, there are only two females on these lists. *Two.* Even for the female identifying . . . there were only two females in total. Finally, female identifying participants were more likely to endorse liking for our most hated characters.

All in all, fascinating results, but they created more questions than they answered. We needed more information. We needed more characters, more inclusivity, and more measures. So that's what we've done. One study at a time. Each one unlocking its own set of mysteries. chapter 2 adds superpowers, chapter 3 explores antiheroes, chapter 5 explores love, chapter 6 focuses on women, and chapter 9 begins to explore fandoms. And we aren't even finished there. Stick around for chapter 10 where we talk about the things yet to be and the things we were doing while writing this book.

Table 1.1. Interpretation of Big Five Scores

High Openness —Imaginative	Low Openness —Practical, Concrete
High Conscientiousness —Disciplined, Organized	Low Conscientiousness —Spontaneous
High Extraversion —Outgoing, Enthusiastic	Low Extraversion —Quiet, Introverted
High Agreeableness —Helpful, Sympathetic	Low Agreeableness —Distrustful, Antagonistic
High Neuroticism (Emotional Stability) —Easily stressed, upset	Low Neuroticism (Emotional Stability) —Calm, Level-headed

REFERENCES

Adams, D. K. (1954). The anatomy of personality. In D. K. Adams (Ed.), *Doubleday papers in psychology* (pp. 1–44). New York, NY: Doubleday & Co.

Burger, J. M. (2017). *Personality, 10th Ed.* Boston, MA: Cengage.

Buhrmester, M. D., Kwang, T., and Gosling, S. D. (2011). Amazon's mechanical turk: A new source of inexpensive, yet high quality data? *Perspectives on Psychological Science, 6,* 3–5.

Costa, P. T., and McCrae, R. R. (1985). *The NEO personality inventory manual.* Odessa, FL: Psychological Assessment Resources.

Danesi, M. (2012). *Introductory perspectives on popular culture: Second edition.* Lanham, MD: Rowman & Littlefield Publishers, Inc.

Digman, J. M. (1997); Higher-order factors of the Big Five. *Journal of Personality and Social Psychology, 73*(6), pp. 1246–1256.

Goldberg, L., and Rosolack, T. (1994). The big five factor structure as an integrative framework: An empirical comparison with Eysenck's P-E-N model. In. C. F. Halverson, Jr., G. A. Kohnstamm, and R. P. Martin (Eds.), *The developing structure of temperament and personality from infancy to adulthood* (pp. 7–35). New York, New York: Erlbaum.

Gosling, S. D., Vazire, S., Srivastava, S., and John, O. P. (2004). Should we trust web-based studies? A comparative analysis of six preconceptions about Internet questionnaires. *American Psychologist, 59,* 93–104.

IBM Corp. Released 2010. IBM SPSS Statistics for Windows, Versions 19.0–25.0. Armonk, NY: IBM Corp.

John, O. P., Robins, R. W., and Pervin, L. A. (2008). *Personality theory and research, 3rd ed.* New York, NY: Guilford.

John, O. P., and Srivastava, S. (1999). The Big-Five trait taxonomy: History, measurement, and theoretical perspectives. In L. A. Pervin and O. P. John (Eds.). *Handbook of personality: Theory and research* (Vol. 2, pp. 102–138). New York: Guilford Press.

Kraaykamp, G., and van Eijck, K. (2005). Personality, media preferences, and cultural participation. *Personality and Individual Differences, 38*, 1675–1688.

Pearce, P. (2003). Psychoanalytic/psychodynamic developmental theories. In V. Simanowitz and P. Pearce (Eds)., Personality Development (pp. 1–29). Berkshire, UK: Open University Press.

Peters, J., Phillips, L., Tull, T. (Producers), and Snyder, Z. (Director). 2013. *Man of Steel* [Motion Picture]. United States: Warner Bros. Pictures.

Qualtrics software, Version XM of Qualtrics. Copyright © 2018 Qualtrics. Qualtrics and all other Qualtrics product or service names are registered trademarks or trademarks of Qualtrics, Provo, UT, USA. (http://www.qualtrics.com).

Rammstedt, B., and John, O. P. (2007). Measuring personality in one minute or less: A 10-item short version of the Big Five Inventory in English and German. *Journal of Research in Personality, 41*, 203–212.

SPSS Inc. Released 2009. PASW Statistics for Windows, Version 18.0. Chicago: SPSS Inc.

Chapter Two

From Superheroes to Superpowers

Superheroes are where we started with our research. We are all fans of super-heroes, and so are many of our participants from what we saw in the results from the previous chapter. Despite including a variety of pop culture charac-ters, our top ten most liked characters included popular superheroes like Bat-man (*DC Universe*), Iron Man (*Marvel Universe*), and Professor X (*Marvel Universe*). Not only did we see these comic book powerhouses who all have wicked powers (well, at least Professor X . . . the other two could be seen as billionaires with lots of toys), but we saw other characters with powers and abilities rounding out the top ten list. It spoke of an interest in powers and abilities outside of the mundane. It definitely piqued our interest and brought up the question of "what superpower do you want?"

Superpowers, in essence, allow our favorites to do their jobs, to save the day. Would Superman (*DC Universe*) be able to rescue Metropolis without his ability to fly? How would Captain America (*Marvel Universe*) save the day without his super strength? Or Legion (*Marvel Universe*) defeat the vil-lain without his power of telepathy? Their powers allow them to take care of business and put the bad guys away . . . something they are supposed to do. After all, that is their job.

Gregory (2015) described how our careers are a part of our identity. We spend so much of our life at work, how can our occupation not influence our identity and perceptions? It is not unusual for you to meet someone for the first time and ask, "what do you do for a living?" Our job can give people indications about our personality, values, priorities, political views, economic standing, and social status. Not only that, but our work is key to our personal well-being. It influences our physical, psychological, and spiritual health. Just think about being in a job for 40+ hours a week that you hate and makes you miserable. How do you think that would impact you and your well-being?

Working in an academic setting, seeing students struggle with occupational choices is a common occurrence. Gregory (2015) supported this notion by adding that career choice is further confounded by the ever-changing global outlook. People who entered the workforce 40 years ago (yes, that would be college graduates in the 1980s) would never have thought that the Internet and technological advances would revolutionize the world in the way that it has. It was a huge deal when you got a wireless phone in 1985. Now, we are talking to people through our watches and carry a mini-computer (i.e., your phone) in our pocket or purse everywhere we go. As a result of globalization of the world's economies, students must be more flexible in the career paths that they pursue. How do we help them? Well, this looks like a *job* for . . .

We wanted to study how a person's choice of superpower might be related to their career selection, interests, and hobbies. For example, does your interest in nature indicate a desired superpower to be able to communicate with animals? What if we knew what superpower you wanted, could that help us predict what job might interest you? So, we developed a study to examine this topic, which we will get into shortly.

First, we need to give you a little background into the theory behind career selection and career interest inventories. This will lead us into a review of the specific measures that we used for our study and why. The stage theories of career development proposed by Super (1953; 1994) investigated career choice through a life-span development model. This theory posits that people differ in their interests, abilities, and personalities. As a result, most people were competent and capable to do many occupations, and these choices can evolve over time and with experience. Think about the careers a child might want to have when they grow up (e.g., astronaut, fire fighter, superhero). Teens explore other career interests and start to think more about how their skills, talents, and values may work together in various potential job opportunities. College students often start out in one major and after taking a few classes in that area decide that this career path is not for them and change again. Adults who have been in a career for several years might decide to make a change in their career path due to the economy, happiness, or other life circumstances that prompt the change.

Gregory (2015) mentions the social cognitive approaches to career choice. This theory proposes that people learn and develop attitudes about careers based on social contexts, observation, and modeling. For example, there are social barriers that result in lack of opportunities for certain groups of people. Sadly, our resources are not equally divided among everyone. While we would like to think that in the land of the free and home of the brave everyone has the same opportunities and options available to them, sadly, this is not the reality. As a result, each person has a unique path to his/her/their career journey.

The theory of person-environment correspondence scrutinizes a person's abilities and matches those abilities to various occupations. Gregory (2015) noted that one's personal values are also important to consider in this theory. Values include altruism involving service to others; autonomy and being independent; comfort level and not feeling stress; and status or recognition that comes from a job. The more that a job corresponds to a person's values the more likely he/she/they will be satisfied and productive within that career.

This leads us into the theory of person-environment *fit*, which explores the relationship between personality type and abilities in relationship to work environment (Dawis, 1996; 2002). John Holland developed the framework for this theory, which resulted in the Holland Codes (1963; Folsom, 1969; Holland and Lutz, 1967; Holland, Whitney, Cole, and Richards, 1969). His theory of vocation choices assumes that a person's selection of a particular vocation is based on heredity, the culture, and personal factors such as friendships, parents, and the physical environment. Each person seeks out and is attracted to an occupational environment that is associated with the person's personality. We particularly liked this theory since it easily related to the trait theory of personality that we have used for our studies. Holland felt that people's interests and work environments, and ultimately what many would call personality, could be loosely divided up into six categories. If you like activities or have similar interests as those in one of those six categories then you would fall under that category (or categories, if you match to more than one), and this would result in your Holland Code. While most people and jobs are best represented by two to three combinations of the six categories, we strictly looked at people's highest code/category in our research.

These categories, which can be abbreviated as RIASEC, are based on the first initial of each of the six categories and will be reviewed below (Holland, 1963).

REALISTIC

These are the Doers. People who are identified as "Realistic" tend to use their physical skills to create a product or service. They often like to work with tools and machinery, plants, and animals. They are interested in the function and purpose of objects. Additionally, these people often like outdoor activities and are athletic. They value tradition, practicality, and common sense. They may like to do things such as fix a car or tinker with machines, go camping, play a sport, or hook up an entertainment center. Common occupations may include airline pilot, farmer, fire fighter, geologist, plumber, and truck driver. A pop culture character that may fit this category is James Howlett/ Logan (aka Wolverine [*Marvel Universe*]).

INVESTIGATIVE

These are the Thinkers. People who are identified as "Investigative" usually like to figure things out and often use logic and reasoning to solve problems. They are observant and enjoy the challenge of problem-solving. They enjoy working with ideas and theories, especially in the scientific realm. These people also like mysteries and situations which involve strategy. They tend to have critical minds, value learning, are curious, and are open to new experienced, ideas, and solutions. They may like to do things such as use a microscope or work in a lab, visit a science museum, study other cultures, or evaluate a crime scene. Common occupations may include astronomer, chemical engineer, computer programmer, historian, biologist, and researcher. A pop culture character that may fit this category is Bruce Banner (aka the Hulk's alter ego [*Marvel Universe*]).

ARTISTIC

These are the Creators. People who are identified as "Artistic" tend to be self-expressive and need to be creative in their activities. They may have an original style and don't conform to the norm or rules. They are sensitive, emotional, and very expressive. They value beauty, originality, and imagination. They may like to do things such as write stories, play an instrument, decorate or draw, take photographs, or entertain. Common occupations may include chef, artist, entertainer/performer, interior decorator, model, and web designer. A pop culture character that may fit this category is photographer, Peter Parker (aka Spider-Man [*Marvel Universe*]).

SOCIAL

These are the Helpers. People who are classified as "Social" like to be around others and tend to want to make a positive difference in the world. They are concerned about the welfare of others and focused on human relationships. They easily relate to all kinds of people and are seen as warm, friendly, and immediately make others feel at home. They could also be involved in teaching, informing, and enlightening others. They value cooperation, generosity, and service to others. They may like to do things such as teach, talk about feelings and provide support, help people with problems, give first aid, or minister to others. Common occupations may include counselor, day care worker, nurse, religious leader, teacher, and speech pathologist. A pop culture character that may fit this category is teacher and principal, Jefferson Pierce (aka Black Lightning [*DC Universe*]).

ENTERPRISING

These are the Persuaders. People who are classified as "Enterprising" are often socially bold, have good verbal skills, and try to persuade others. They typically take on leadership roles and are assertive and adventurous. This type of person may enjoy being the focus of attention. They tend to value risk taking, status, competition, and influence. They may like to do things such as sell goods, debate a topic, manage a business or organization, or read about current events. Common occupations may include lawyer, manager, politician, realtor, promoter, reporter, and salesperson. A pop culture character that may fit this category is entrepreneur, Lex Luthor (*DC Universe*).

CONVENTIONAL

These are the Organizers. People who are identified as "Conventional" enjoy working with facts and figures, record keeping, and are very organized. They are often methodical, precise, and detail oriented. They like to know the chain of command and have well-defined instructions for their tasks. They tend to focus on practical issues and do not get lost in fantasy. They value accuracy, stability, and efficiency. They may like to do things such as clean and organize, sort the mail, create a budget and keep accurate records, write reports, and make charts, tables, and graphs. Common occupations may include accountant, bookkeeper, bank teller, editor, office manager, records clerk, and secretary. A pop culture character that may fit this category is the editor of the *Daily Planet*, Perry White (*DC Universe*).

There are numerous career evaluation tools and some are better than others. You can find Buzzfeed, Reddit, and Facebook quizzes that claim to help you with career selection, but these are often only for entertainment purposes. There are some other, more psychologically sound instruments with solid reliability and validity to back their results. Krumboltz (1994) created the Career Beliefs Inventory (CBI). This instrument was made to increase awareness of a person's beliefs about a particular occupation and the bidirectional relationship between that and a person's life satisfaction. The test is 96 items and results in 25 scales. While this would be very useful for some situations, it was deemed to be too detailed and extensive for what we wanted to do for our study.

There are several other tests that explore people's interests. These include the Strong Interest Inventory-Revised, the Self-Directed Search, and the Campbell Interest and Skill Inventory (Gregory, 2015). These measures include almost 300 to over 400 items and, in addition to the number of other items in our study, we had concerns that participants would become fatigued, begin randomly answering items, or skip items. Likewise, while interests are a part of what we wanted to examine, we were more curious about career interests and therefore decided to not use any of these measures.

For our study, we created a job interest inventory based on Holland's (Holland and Lutz, 1967) occupational themes. Participants rated specific jobs/occupations on a scale of 1 to 7 (extremely dislike to extremely like) as to how much each job appealed to the participants. There was also a list of qualities related to jobs, such as the person's hobbies/interests, attributes or qualities the participants felt they held, and their perceived level of skill proficiency at various tasks. Participants rated these items on a scale of 0 to 6 (strongly disagree to strongly agree) as to how each item applied to them. We then examined the pattern of responses to score the participant's answers under the different occupational areas: Realistic, Investigative, Artistic, Social, Enterprising, and Conventional. A general issue with most all career interest inventories, including our own, is that fact that the questions often reflect cognitive abilities, intellectual skills, and physical talents. These tests often overlook emotional problems, which could include dysfunctional thoughts about career choices that could hamper career development (Krumboltz, 1993).

Participants were also provided with a list of over 200 superheroes and villains from television, film, and comics (similar to the list constructed in chapter 1–more details about this in appendix B). They were asked to go through the list and rate each character on a scale of one to seven as to the degree to which they "liked" the characters (1 = Strongly dislike, while 7 = Strongly like). This scale marked a departure from chapter 1 in two ways. First, we expanded the scale from "one to five" to "one to seven." Secondly, we dropped the "identify" measure as it did not produce any differences from the "like" measure. We did allow for individuals to skip (and not rate) characters that they did not know. Participants were also given a list of 60 superpowers and asked to rate the powers based on how much they "liked" the power (1 = Strongly dislike, while 7 = Strongly like). We also asked them to choose the one power that they most wanted. As with chapter 1 (and in all studies moving forward with a couple of exceptions) we used three primary tools to collect this dataset and distribute our survey: Amazon's Mechanical Turk (MTurk), SONA, and Qualtrics (http://www.qualtrics.com) (Qualtrics, Provo, UT).

Our sample consisted of 411 participants ranging in age from 18 to 72. (See appendix A for more information about the types of demographic information that we collected about our sample.) Fifty-eight percent self-identified as female, and 41 percent self-identified as male. The majority of our sample was Caucasian and had a bachelor's degree or some college. Fifty-two percent were employed, with 15 percent reporting that they were self-employed. Seventy-six percent of the participants considered themselves to be fans of superhero-related media.

When participants were asked to choose which power that they would "most want" they chose Invisibility (11.4 percent), Time Travel (8 percent), Teleportation (7.8 percent), Immortality (7.8 percent), and Flight (7.3 percent) as the top five. However, when we asked participants to rate how much they "liked" each individual superpower, these were not the ones that came out on top. In order, the most "liked" (not selected as wanted) superpowers were Super Intelligence, Healing Factor, Flight, Teleportation, Time Travel, Invisibility, Super Strength, Telekinesis, Super Speed, Endurance, and Telepathy. The least liked powers were Claws, Sonic Scream, Feeding on Life Energy, Concussive Blast, Spider Powers, Plant Control, Cybernetics, Elasticity, Robot/Android Powers, and Immovability.

In general, the superpowers that are most liked are positively correlated to the superheroes who are most liked. Likewise, the superpowers that are least liked are correlated to the superheroes/villains who are least liked. In general, the most liked superpowers are NOT correlated (related) to the least liked superheroes/villains, and the least liked superpowers are not correlated (related) to the most liked superheroes. In addition, while occupational interest and career scores are predictive of the superpowers that we like, they are NOT predictive of the superheroes/villains that we like. So, do we pick our favorite heroes, or do we pick our favorite powers?

When we examined our measures related to Holland's (1963) codes and our participants, we found that there was a pattern in what superpower a participant liked and falling into a certain Holland Code. Those interested in the powers of Radar and Claws fell into the Realistic Holland Code. There was some overlap in certain powers as well. For example, the power of Radar was also of interest to those who fell into the Investigative and the Conventional Holland Codes. Looking further at Investigative, in addition to Radar, having interest in powers such as Magnetic Manipulation, Invisibility, and being a Cosmic Being/God were predictive of being placed in that code. Likewise, in addition to Radar, the people who liked Super Strength and Power Tech/

Armor were attracted to the Conventional Holland Code. Those who were interested in the superpowers Water Breathing, Protective Form, Concussive Blast, Animal Powers, and Healing placed in the Artistic Holland Code. Those interested in the superpowers Super Hearing, Precognition, Mystical Arts/Magic, and Plant Control were drawn to the Social Holland Code. Finally, if the superpowers Sonic Scream, Super Hearing, Illusion Casting, Precognition, and Spider Powers were liked, these people fell into the Enterprising Holland Code. Based on these finding, asking a person what their desired/liked superpower would be can give us an indication of which Holland Code the person is interested in.

We then looked at things from the opposite point of view (which predicts which?). Instead of examining what superpower a person liked and seeing how that might draw them toward a particular Holland code, we wanted to know if the Holland Code, itself, would predict what superpowers a person would have interest in. It did!

Those who were identified as Investigative predict interests in these powers: Animal Control, Time Travel, and Teleportation. This is interesting because those who fall into this code, as mentioned earlier, are the Thinkers. People in this code like things related to science. The powers they selected are relevant to scientific fields such as physics, biology, and chemistry. We can see this play out in Barry Allen (aka the Flash [*DC Universe*]), who is a scientist for the police and through his power of speed can time travel.

Being identified as Artistic predicts interests in: Animal Control, Animal Powers, Illusion Casting, Precognition, Magic, and Water Breathing. This is interesting since those in the Artistic category are referred to as the Creators. Casting illusion, precognition, and magic are all very creative and make one think of the "artsy-hippie" person. Likewise, having animal powers and the ability to breathe under water would give a person a new perspective of the world, which is often what artists do for society. This is illustrated with Kyle Rayner (aka Green Lantern [*DC Universe*]), who is an artist in his everyday life, but as Green Lantern can cast illusions/constructs by wielding his lantern ring.

Being identified as Social predicts interests in Invulnerability and Time Travel. This did not surprise us since these people are considered the Helpers. Being invulnerable would shield the helpers from harm while they work to protect others. Likewise, if they could time travel, they would be able to stop bad things from happening and as a result, help others make better choices or have a more positive future. Jean Grey of the X-Men demonstrates a great deal of empathy as she works with the students at the Xavier School for the Gifted.

Being identified as Enterprising predicts interests in Immortality, Luck, Time Travel, Spider Powers, and Steel Skin. Since these are the Persuaders and often business people, having several of these powers would be useful. Luck would help with promoting and selling things, steel skin would relate to having a "thick skin" when rejection occurs, and being immortal or having the ability to time travel would potentially help one generate a mass of wealth. Who wouldn't want to go back in time and buy some Apple stock? The villain, Vandal Savage (*DC Universe*), is not only immortal but has amassed great wealth, resources, and knowledge.

Being identified as Conventional only predicts interests in Sharp-Shooting. Since these are the Organizers, it is not surprising that they would like a superpower that relates to precision and accuracy. Peggy Carter (*Marvel Universe*) initially started out working in an office, typical for women during her time. As she moved up through the ranks and ultimately became a founding member of SHIELD, she developed a steady arm and was a good shot.

As an interesting side note, while occupational interests and career scores are predictive of the superpowers that we like, they are NOT predictive of the superheroes/villains that we like. Those were separate entities in that respect. Just as we saw with our previous chapter, you like whom you like. The superhero you like does not necessarily reflect your preferred superpower, nor is it based on the superpower you like per se. Just because you love Daredevil (*Marvel Universe*) does not mean you love enhanced sense, nor does it mean your love of the power to shapeshift mean that you like Beast Boy (*DC Universe*).

However, using our strengths and interests can help us find the career path that suits us best and where we can do the most good. We spend so much of our lives working, it is important that we find something to do that is meaningful and engaging. Superheroes and their abilities are aspirational. Perhaps they even provide us with a form of wish fulfillment. "We live in the stories we tell ourselves . . . superhero stories speak loudly and boldly to our greatest fears, deepest longings, and highest aspirations" (Morrison, 2011, p. xvii).

REFERENCES

Dawis, R. V. (1996). The theory of work adjustment and person-environment correspondence counseling. In D. Brown and L. Brooks (Eds.), *Career choice and development* (3rd ed., pp. 75–120). San Francisco: Jossey-Bass.

Dawis, R. V. (2002). Person-Environment Correspondence theory. In D. Brown and Associates (Eds.), *Career choice and development* (4th ed., pp. 427–464). San Francisco: Jossey-Bass.

Folsom, Jr., C. H. (1969). An investigation of Holland's theory of vocational choice. *Journal of Counseling Psychology, 16*(3), 260–266.

Gregory, R. J. (2015). *Psychological testing: History, principles, and applications*, 7th edition–global edition. Boston, MA: Pearson.

Holland, J. L. (1963). Explorations of a theory of vocational choice and achievement. II. A four-year prediction study. *Psychological Reports, 12*, 547–594.

Holland, J. L., and Lutz, S. W. (1967). Predicting a student's vocational choice. *ACT Research Report, 18*, 3–25.

Holland, J. L., Whitney, D. R., Cole, N. S., and Richards, Jr., J. M. (1969). An empirical occupational classification from a theory of personality and intended for practice and research. *ACT Research Report, 29*, 5–29.

Krumboltz, J. D. (1993). Integrating career and personal counseling. *Career Development Quarterly, 42*, 143–148.

Krumboltz, J. D. (1994). The Career Beliefs Inventory. *Journal of Counseling and Development*, 72(4), 424–428.

Morrison, G. (2011). *Supergods*. New York, New York Spiegel & Grau.

Qualtrics Software, Version XM of Qualtrics. Copyright © 2018 Qualtrics. Qualtrics and all other Qualtrics product or service names are registered trademarks or trademarks of Qualtrics, Provo, UT, USA. (http://www.qualtrics.com).

Super, D. E. (1953). A theory of vocational development. *American Psychologist, 8*(5), 185–190.

Super, D. E. (1994). A life-span, life-space perspective on convergence. In M. L. Savickas and R. W. Lent (Eds.), *Convergence in career development theories: Implications for science and practice* (pp. 63–74). Palo Alto, CA: CPP Books.

Chapter Three

What about the Bad Guys?

Pop culture is largely stories. Those stories matter and take many forms as we saw across the progress of our research. In fact, we saw a rise of specific stories not long after we started working on our initial projects. Darth Vader (*Rogue One: A Star Wars Story*) slashed across the screen in 2016, his red lightsaber cutting through rebels and sending chills through movie goers. The Sith Lord was back and introduced a new level of fear to fans (Kennedy, Shearmur, Emanuel, and Edwards, 2016). A few months prior, the Joker's (*DC Universe*) maniacal laugh had filled theaters once more with the release of *Suicide Squad* (Roven, Suckle, and Ayer, 2016), and Deadpool (*Marvel Universe*) had smashed the box offices just before that with his katanas, tacos, and sarcasm (Kinberg, Reynolds, Donner, and Miller, 2016). It was the year of the villains and the antiheroes. In a world of Thors (*Marvel Universe)*, people were turning their attention to the Lokis (*Marvel Universe*) instead, and so too were we.

With the popularity of villains seemingly on the rise, we wanted to know more about what was driving the love to hate (and to love) relationship fans had with these characters. As you know by now, we included several villains and antiheroes alongside our heroes in previous studies. In doing so, we started to see trends within personality traits and people's love (or hate) for different characters. It left us wondering if there would be differences in those who love a "true" hero compared to a "true" villain compared to the antihero in the "middle" position. For example, how would traits differ for those who like *Star Wars* characters such as Luke Skywalker (hero) compared to Darth Vader (villain) compared to Han Solo (antihero) (Kurtz and Lucas, 1977)?

We wanted to explore how people would view these very different characters, and previous research has indicated differences between these tropes (heroes, villains, and antiheroes). Most consider the hero to be the classic good guy. A hero tends to exhibit positive characteristics and, according to Rosch, exhibits more morality, warmth, and honesty than the average character (as cited in Grizzard, Huang, Fitzgerald, Ahn, and Chu, 2018). A villain, according to this, is the opposite to the hero in most characteristics. The villain is more likely to violate morality, harm others, and lie for his/her own gain (Grizzard et al., 2018).

Additionally, previous research has demonstrated differences in how villains and heroes look. Traditionally speaking, a hero is the dashing lead. They tend to be portrayed by attractive actors or are drawn with more favorable characteristics, whereas the villains tend to look darker and are less attractive in some way to the viewers (Grizzard et al., 2018). This striking difference can be seen with the original *Star Wars* trilogy (Kurtz and Lucas, 1977; Kurtz and Kershner, 1980; Kazanjian and Marquand, 1983). Luke Skywalker is the light to Darth Vader's dark, in more ways than just their use of force. With Mark Hamill portraying the handsome, blonde-haired hero, there is a stark contrast in looks between him and Darth Vader's monstrous appearance in his black mask and cape (Kurtz and Lucas, 1977). The hero is portrayed as a handsome character whereas the villain is almost grotesque in appearance, giving physical clues to the audience in addition to the storyline.

However, over time and with the rise of the antiheroes, the line between hero and villain has become more muddled. A character classified as an antihero is typically darker in nature than their traditional counterparts yet work toward a greater good . . . most of the time. The characters are more flawed and ambiguous in their presentation (Eden, Daalmans, and Johnson, 2017). The audience typically understands what a hero's goal is throughout their arc, whereas an antihero may change frequently from one movie or comic pane to the next. This can be seen through the journey of Tony Stark/Iron Man (*Marvel Universe*) in the recent Marvel Cinematic Universe films. In Arad, Feige, and Favreau's 2008 *Iron Man*, the audience heard Tony Stark say "I'm not the hero type" before boastingly revealing himself to be Iron Man. Cut to 2019 (spoiler alert ahead!), the audience sees Tony make the ultimate sacrifice for the greater good (Feige, Russo, and Russo, 2019).

Antiheroes depict a different breed of character, one who can be traditionally heroic in some instances and traditionally villainous in others. This can make it difficult to see which character clearly fits into which mold. The hero, villain, and antihero schemas rely on audience perception and can vary in some instances due to different views of morality and consciousness for audience members (Eden, Daalmans, and Johnson, 2017). Researchers have gone so far as to label antiheroes as having personality traits such as narcissism, much like what is seen with the often-beloved Tony Stark mentioned above (Jonason, Webster, Schmitt, Li, and Crysel, 2012). This became important for us in regard to our study and gave us a new direction in which to take our measures.

Additionally, as we looked across the Internet at how people viewed character tropes, we began to notice that the gaming alignment chart was a "frequent flyer" in the world of online personality measures as well as with memes for fandoms, highlighting the good, the bad, and the ugly with a specific show. This alignment chart, which is a combination of personal morality and attitudes, breaks individuals or characters into levels of *morality* in terms of good, evil, or neutral, and in terms of the *attitudes* of lawful, chaotic, or neutral ("Alignment," n.d.). An alignment chart utilizes nine squares (three rows of three) and organizes based on how one views and abides by "the law" (Andersen, 2016). When creating characters in a game such as Dungeons and Dragons (DnD) (Gygax and Arneson, 2014), for example, the player looks at how his/her characters fits along the good, neutral, and evil spectrum. It considers how the character follows along a path of good or evil, is lawful or chaotic, or is truly neutral in their acts ("Alignment," n.d.). Although it was made famous in the gaming world, fans frequently utilize these terms to categorize their favorite characters.

With the focus on the dark side of pop culture characters and the morally ambiguous, it seemed fitting to add to our personality measures and focus on the dark side of that as well. McCrae and John's Big Five (1992) theory measured through the Big Five Inventory (BFI) (John and Srivastava, 1999) had allowed us to see differences in those who preferred heroes to villains in our previous studies. Yet, the Big Five does not cover all areas of personality. Like the Big Five, the trait-based theory known as the Dark Triad aims to study normal, although seemingly more malevolent, personality traits. As the name suggests, this theory is comprised of three separate dimensions, all of which have some correlations to the others in terms of the characteristics and behaviors seen in individuals. These traits consist of Machiavellianism, narcissism, and psychopathy (Jonason, Kavanagh, Webster, and Fitzgerald, 2011).

Machiavellianism is often considered a manipulative personality type that is characterized as someone who acts in a cold manner and manipulates others for their own gains (Paulhus and Williams, 2002). A prime example of Machiavellianism can be seen in the *Game of Thrones* character Lord Baelish (aka Littlefinger, who does everything he does for his own power gain at the cost of friends and those he loves (Benioff and Weiss, 2019). Although the narcissism trait shares its name with a disorder classified in the Diagnostic and Statistical Manual of Mental Disorders (DSM-5; American Psychiatric Association, 2013), it is not of clinical significance nor is it diagnostic, like its counterpart. However, it does share similarities in terms of the characteristics associated with this trait, such as feelings of grandiosity and superiority. Paulhus and Williams (2002) discuss how individuals with this trait tend to have a sense of entitlement over others and act in a more dominating manner compared to most. As we have said, Tony Stark is frequently depicting this traits in comic and movie lore (Arad, Feige, and Favreau, 2008). Finally, psychopathy is usually a trait defined by high impulsivity and lack of empathy for others. A character who possesses this trait tends to be someone who seeks thrills and experiences low amounts of anxiety (Paulhus and Williams, 2002). The villainous Joker has been traditionally touted as having psychopathic traits, especially in Christopher Nolan's *Dark Knight* film (Nolan, Thomas, and Roven, 2008).

In these three traits one can see vast differences when compared to those of the Big Five traits. Statistical analysis of the traits has demonstrated that many of the Dark Triad traits are negatively correlated to the Big Five traits (Yetişer, 2014). For example, narcissism and Machiavellianism are negatively correlated to agreeableness and conscientiousness. That is not to say that there are no overlaps, however. For example, there is no statistically significant correlation between some of the constructs, such as psychopathy and openness (Jakobwitz and Egan, 2006). These results suggest that there are significant differences between the Dark Triad and the Big Five traits that justify the use of both theories (and measures) in this study.

Although this research does suggest important differences in terms of characteristics across the Big Five and the Dark Triad, that is not to say that there are not important similarities. Much like the Big Five, there are certain behaviors associated with the Dark Triad. Researchers have found behavioral patterns across all three aspects of the triad that indicate similarities, including a general disagreeableness and a lack of humility (Jonason, Kavanagh, Webster, and Fitzgerald, 2011). However, there are also differences between the traits of the Dark Triad that warrant an examination of each construct individually. Machiavellianism, narcissism, and psychopathy lend to differences in terms of both behaviors and emotions. Differences regarding impulse control and risk-taking activities have been found among the three dimensions (Jonason et al., 2011). Jones and Paulhus (2011) found that both narcissism and psychopathy were found in impulsive individuals, who are prone to act without considering the consequences. These researchers, however, did not find this behavior in individuals who scored highly on the Machiavellianism trait. Furthermore, high psychopathy scores are associated more with risk-taking behaviors (unsafe sex, alcohol/drug use, etc.) whereas high narcissism scores tend to be associated with social and outgoing behaviors (Jonason, Baughman, Carter, and Parker, 2015). These studies suggest that each trait on the triad represents subtle differences on the continuum regarding behaviors.

As previously mentioned, these traits do not reflect diagnostic criteria, despite the fact that some, such as narcissism and psychopathy, share names and details similar to specific diagnoses (Paulhus and Williams, 2002; Jakobwitz and Egan, 2006). Opposed to personality disorders, these personality dimensions can reflect normal, albeit sometimes seemingly aversive, aspects of personality (Yetişer, 2014). Rather, the theories discussed are indicators of traits the individual possess that might only warrant further examination for clinical diagnosis. Measures that indicate personality disorders or more clinical diagnostic criteria were not used for the purpose of this study and are outside of our scope of discussion.

Instead, we chose instruments that have been designed to determine what characteristics tend to be associated with one personality trait over another for both the Big Five and the Dark Triad. Much like personality theories in general, it has long been debated as to what measures are the best indicators of personality. Many researchers have developed and tested a variety of instruments hoping to ascertain what the best reflection of personality traits are.

Unlike the BFI (John and Srivastava, 1999), which measures all five of the Big Five traits, most research surrounding ways to measure the Dark Triad have examined concepts through a multi-instrument approach for each of the three traits. Measures such as the Self Report Psychopathy Scale (SRP-III) (Paulhus, Neumann, and Hare, 2009), the Test of Machiavellianism (MACH-IV) (Yetişer, 2014), and the Narcissistic Personality Inventory (NPI) (Raskin and Hall, 1981) have all been developed and researched as valid instruments that can be used to assess Dark Triad related personalities. Although the debate continues as to what is truly the best manner by which to measure personality traits, the following have been shown to be both valid and reliable methods of identifying personality traits from individuals.

The Self Report Psychopathy Scale (SRP-III) is traditionally used as a way to measure the trait of psychopathy. This 64-item instrument allows researchers to determine traits related to interpersonal manipulation, callous affect, erratic lifestyle, and antisocial behavior; these subscales provide a way to assess for the personality trait. By scoring and averaging the subscales, one can determine how highly an individual rates on overall psychopathy (Paulhus, Neumann, and Hare, 2009). Furthermore, the measure has been found to be reliable (alpha reliability up to .90) (Gordts, Uzieblo, Neumann, Van den Bussche, and Rossi, 2015). As such, it has been used in a variety of studies regarding areas of interest such as criminality and aggression (as cited in Gordts et al., 2015, p. 1).

In 1970, Christie and Geis developed a measure to rate Machiavellianism characteristics, referred to as the MACH-IV scale. This 20-item instrument includes statements for participants to read; individuals then rate the degree to which they disagree or agree with the opinion or implication of each. The more a person agrees with statements, the higher the score and the more it lends to a higher level of Machiavellian thoughts and traits (as cited in Yetişer, 2014, p. 6331). Jones and Paulhus determined that this measure was a reliable instrument to measure Machiavellianism (Cronbach's alpha 0.83) (as cited in Yetişer, 2014, p. 6331). It has also been described as being a valid measurement of traits associated with Machiavellianism (Fehr, Samson, and Paulhus, 1992).

Multiple assessments have been developed as ways to measure traits related to narcissism, for both clinical and research-related purposes. The Minnesota Multiphasic Personality Inventory-II (MMPI-2) is frequently used as a way to assess for disordered personality and more adverse characteristics that would interfere with daily functioning (Watson and Biderman, 1993). Although the MMPI-2 is very reliable and valid, it can be cumbersome to use in research given its length and complexity, and we ultimately did not want to measure diagnostic criteria for the purposes of this study. Again, diagnostic instruments and criteria are not related to traits but instead disorders, which we did not want to measure.

Raskin and Hall (1981) developed the Narcissistic Personality Inventory (NPI) as a simpler, self-report measure of narcissistic attitudes. This 40-item instrument forces participants to choose between a pair of "I" statements. The individual chooses which statement is the best descriptor for him or herself. One statement in each pair lends to the notion of a heightened sense of self. Such statements include "Modesty doesn't become me" and "If I ruled the world it would be a better place." These statements are scored higher than the others. Higher scores lend to what can be considered a narcissist thought pattern (as cited in Watson and Biderman, 1993, p. 42). Additionally, it is a valid indicator of narcissism traits, especially grandiosity (Rosenthal, Montoya, Ridings, Rieck, and Hooley, 2011). By using all of these measures in one study, it is believed that the researchers will gain a better and broader understanding of participants' personality traits across the continuum.

Participants responded to items from the BFI (John and Srivastava, 1999) as well as the previously mentioned Dark Triad instruments. They also responded to several demographic items (see appendix A for a discussion of these). After completing personality measures, they responded to the list of over 400 characters. *Yes, 400 characters* (see appendix B for a discussion of these). We all had a hand in who we believed needed to be on the list, and this drove up the numbers. The characters ranged from comic books to literature to film and television. The characters represented a variety of genres, including superhero media, science fiction, and fantasy. They also came from a variety of publishers and production companies, such as Disney, Marvel, HBO, DC, and many others.

After obtaining over 600 participants (via Qualtrics [http://www.qualtrics.com] [Qualtrics, Provo, UT], Amazon MTurk [MTurk, www.MTurk.com], and the SONA System), we scored each of the personality measures (for a total of eight subscale scores defining openness, conscientiousness, extraversion, agreeableness, neuroticism/emotionally stability, Machiavellianism, narcissism, and psychopathy according to their individual scoring instructions). All results remained anonymous and nothing could be linked back to any one participant who completed the survey. We utilized manipulation checks to ensure participants read items rather than engaged in "Christmas treeing," by clicking random items instead. As we stated earlier, we believed that those who scored highly in one personality dimension over another would, as a whole, prefer specific characters over others. In particular, we believed and wanted to examine if those who scored higher on the Dark Triad traits would prefer the characters traditionally seen as clear-cut villains (i.e., Darth Vader, Joffrey Baratheon [*Game of Thrones*], Dolores Umbridge [*Harry Potter*], etc.). To examine this, we utilized multiple regression analyses with Bonferroni corrections to see how personality traits predicted character interest. A Bonferroni correction was conducted to counter the number of analyses conducted and protect the Type I error rate, and the significance level has been lowered to $p = <.001$ to be significant and $p < .01$ and $p < .005$ are considered marginally significant. We learned a lot.

We ran a series of regression analyses on a specific subset of characters to see how interest in those characters related to the different personality measures. Although not every character was statistically significant, we came across what we considered interesting trends with the characters we would personally consider heroes, antiheroes, and villains. We would like to note that the way we categorized some of the characters could be up for debate. Some would consider Loki (*Marvel Universe*) a true villain (especially if you are more of a comic person) whereas we have him currently listed more as an antihero (thanks, in part, to Tom Hiddleston's portrayal of the flawed character in films), and many would now consider Daenerys Targaryen a villain following the finale season of *Game of Thrones* (Benioff and Weiss, 2019). Fans hold different perceptions of characters, as evidenced by the various blogs and flames throughout Tumblr and Reddit. However, as our data indicates, trends that arose appeared to fit into a specific pattern, and this largely influenced how we then interpreted our characters.

There appeared to be a pattern with the way these characters broke down as we began to analyze. Harkening back to our previous discussion on align-

Table 3.1. Character Alignments

Obi-Wan**	Luke Skywalker**	Sirius Black***
Hermione***	Harry Potter***	Batman*
Spock***	Cap Kirk***	Princess Leia***
Peeta***	Katniss***	Iron Man***
Yoda***	Rey***	Ron Weasley***
	Groot**	Storm***
	Daenerys Targaryen**	
Lawful Good	***Neutral Good***	***Chaotic Good***
Magneto***	Jack Harkness**	Han Solo***
Jar Jar Binks*	Hodor**	Loki**
	Poison Ivy*	Harley Quinn***
	Comm Gordon***	Star Lord*
	Boba Fett**	Doctor Who*
	Black Widow***	
	Winter Soldier *	
Lawful Neutral	***True Neutral***	***Chaotic Neutral***
Darth Vader***	Riddler*	Joker***
Two Face***		Joffrey*
Jabba the Hutt*		
Lex Luthor**		
Lawful Evil	***Neutral Evil***	***Chaotic Evil***

ment, we took a page out of the gamer's handbook and noticed how these characters fit along the chart (see table 3.1). Using the definitions of each aspect we created the following breakdown.

Overall, we found some interesting results. For example, the characters that we identified as more *Lawful Good* all seemed to show a similar pattern where those who indicated that they liked those characters more exhibited higher scores on positive personality traits as defined by the BFI. For example, Obi-Wan (*Star Wars*), Hermione (*Harry Potter*), Spock (*Star Trek*), and Yoda (*Star Wars*) were all associated with higher levels of openness. We hypothesize that it would take a more open person to like space operas and schools of magic. Several of these characters were also associated with lower levels of Dark Triad scores. Hermione (Machiavellianism), Spock (narcissism), and Peeta (also narcissism [*Hunger Games*]) were all associated with these lower Dark Triad scores. In contrast, the more *Lawful Evil* identified characters were *all* associated with higher levels of the Dark Triad, specifically psychopathy. Those who like Darth Vader, Two-Face (*DC Universe*), Jabba the Hutt (*Star Wars*), and Lex Luthor (*DC Universe*) more were all associated with significantly higher scores on psychopathy. Interestingly, Two-Face was also associated with lower levels of narcissism, which left us questioning if one of his "faces" was more inclined toward the Dark Triad while the other was less inclined to meet that dark fate. This was also supported by the idea that Two-Face is also associated with higher levels of openness and agreeableness (Darth Vader and Jabba the Hutt were also associated with openness, which probably speaks to that whole space opera theory that we mentioned earlier).

We also saw similar patterns with *Neutral Good* and *Neutral Evil*. Luke Skywalker, Harry Potter (*Harry Potter*), Captain Kirk (*Star Trek*), Rey (Palpatine or Solo, depending on how you interpret [*Star Wars*]), Groot (*Marvel Universe*), and Daenerys Targaryen were all significantly more liked by individuals who were high on openness (and were not predicted by any higher traits from the Dark Triad) while Riddler (*DC Universe*)—identified here as *Neutral Evil*—was also more liked by individuals identifying as higher on openness but also higher on psychopathy. Interestingly, Katniss Everdeen (*The Hunger Games*), Rey, and Groot were all also more liked by individuals demonstrating *low* levels of narcissism, and Katniss was more liked by individuals who scored higher on extraversion and emotional stability.

Predictably, at this point, *Chaotic Good* and *Chaotic Evil* identified characters followed similar patterns. Higher scores on emotional stability were associated with higher levels of liking for Sirius Black (*Harry Potter*), Princess Leia (along with being more open and less narcissistic [*Star Wars*]), Ron Weasley (*Harry Potter*) and Storm (*Marvel Universe*). Ron Weasley, Storm, and Iron Man (also associated with lower levels of psychopathy) were also associated with higher levels of openness, like Princess Leia.

Batman was the only one to break this pattern, and liking Batman was associated with higher levels of conscientiousness. April always likes to say, "Be like Batman." This is implying that one should always have a back-up plan for one's back-up plan's back-up plan. That seems to fit with the conscientious mindset. It was then interesting for these researchers to see that Joker (representing *Chaotic Evil*) would also be statistically significant and associated with higher levels of psychopathy, openness, and agreeableness. Joffrey Baratheon (or should it really be Lannister?) was also in this category and was more liked by those scoring higher on Machiavellianism, which seems to be of little surprise.

The really interesting thing about this project was not the clean results that we saw between the "good" guys and the "bad." The really interesting results applied to the "neutral" characters . . . those antiheroes that got us started in the first place. Those results were a mixed bag with high and low levels of the Big Five Traits as well as high and low levels on the Dark Triad. In terms of *Lawful Neutral*, more positive views of Magneto (*Marvel Universe*) were associated with higher levels of openness, and Jar Jar Binks

(*Star Wars*) was associated with higher levels of agreeableness and higher levels of emotional stability.

In terms of *True Neutral* (our most hotly internally contested categorizations), higher levels of liking were most associated with higher levels of openness. Jack Harkness (*Doctor Who and Torchwood*), Hodor (*Game of Thrones*) (who was also associated with lower levels of narcissism), Poison Ivy (*DC Universe*) (who was also associated with higher levels of emotional stability, agreeableness, *and* psychopathy), Commissioner Gordon (*DC Universe*) (who, in direct contrast to Batman, was also associated with lower levels of conscientiousness), Black Widow (who was also associated with high levels of emotional stability [*Marvel Universe*]), and Winter Soldier (who was also associated with lower levels of narcissism [*Marvel Universe*]). The only one who did not follow a similar pattern was Boba Fett (*Star Wars*). More liking of Boba Fett was associated with higher levels of agreeableness and psychopathy.

Finally, we come to *Chaotic Neutral*. Every single individual in this group was associated with higher liking scores by those endorsing more openness; in fact, this was the only trait associated with Doctor Who. It should be clarified that at the time of this study, the individual Doctors (i.e., Nine, Ten, Eleven, etc.) were not studied separately; "The Doctor" was instead listed as one character. We have since separated out individual Doctors, however at the time participants could assume whichever Doctor they preferred for the character. Han Solo (also associated with lower levels of Machiavellianism), Loki, and Star Lord (*Marvel Universe*) were all also associated with lower levels of narcissism. We found this particularly interesting as these three researchers would all certainly agree that each of these three characters can come across as narcissistic, themselves. Rounding out this list was Harley Quinn (*DC Universe*). In addition to openness, higher scores for liking Harley were associated with higher levels of emotional stability and higher levels of psychopathy. It is interesting to note that the whole Harley Quinn, Poison Ivy, and Joker triad are all more liked by those with higher levels of psychopathy.

With these results, we could see that individuals who displayed more positive traits of the Big Five and more negative traits on the Dark Triad tend to prefer characters viewed as heroes (i.e., Iron Man: $F(8, 382) = 3.64, p < .001$). Those who display a mix of traits (positive/negative Big Five/Dark Triad) tended to prefer characters viewed as antiheroes (i.e., Harley Quinn: $F(8, 313) = 3.26, p = .001$. and Loki: $F(8, 332) = 3.09, p = .002$). Furthermore, those who displayed positive traits of the Dark Triad tend to prefer villains (i.e., Joker: $F(8, 387) = 5.00, p < .001$). The only exception to this trend was Two-Face, a character who is literally dual natured ($F(8, 314) = 3.78, p < .001$).

As we began to wrap up this study, the Dark Triad was becoming a buzzword in and of itself, much in the way the antihero craze had when we first started. However, as we concluded our study the political scene began dominating not only news, but also popular culture, with many suddenly using words such as narcissism and personality trait. As you will see in future chapters, this drove us to continue to utilize the Dark Triad in a majority of our research. Especially with the trolls . . .

REFERENCES

Alignment: Dnd5e.info: The 5th edition system reference document. (n.d.) https://dnd5e.info/beyond-1st-level/alignment/.

American Psychiatric Association. (2013). *Diagnostic and statistical manual of mental disorders: DSM-5.* Washington, D.C: American Psychiatric Association.

Andersen, K. (2016). The chart that explains everyone. Studio 360. Retrieved from https://www.wnyc.org/story/the-chart-that-explains-everyone-character-alignment/.

Arad, A., and Feige, K., (Producers) and Favreau, J. (Director). (2008). *Iron Man* [Motion Picture]. United States: Paramount Pictures.

Benioff, D., and Weiss, D. (Creators). (2019). *Game of Thrones* [Television Series]. United States: Warner Bros. Television.

Eden, A., Daalmans, S. and Johnsons, B. (2017). Morality predicts enjoyment but not appreciation of morally ambiguous characters. *Media Psychology, 20,* 349–373.

Fehr, B., Samson, D., and Paulhus, D. L. (1992). The construct of Machiavellianism: Twenty years later. In C. D. Spielberger and J. N. Butcher (Eds.), *Advances in personality assessment* (Vol. 9, pp.77–116). Hillsdale, NJ: Erlbaum.

Feige, K. (Producer), Russo, A. and Russo, J. (Directors). (2019). *Avengers: Endgame* [Motion Picture]. United States: Walt Disney Studios.

Gordts, S., Uzieblo, K., Neumann, C., Van den Bussche, E., and Rossi, G. (2015). Validity of the self-report psychopathy scales (SRP-III full and shorter versions) in a community sample. *Assessment, 24*(3), 1–18.

Grizzard, M., Huang, J., Fitzgerald, K., Ahn, C. and Chu, H. (2018). Sensing heroes and villains: Character-schema and the disposition formation process. *Communication Research, 45*(4), 479–501.

Gygax, G. and Arneson, D. (Designers). (2014). *Dungeons & Dragons 5th Edition* [Game]. https://media.wizards.com/2018/dnd/downloads/DnD_BasicRules_2018.pdf.

Jakobwitz, S. and Egan, V. (2006). The Dark Triad and normal personality traits. *Personality and Individual Differences, 40,* 331–339.

John, O. P., and Srivastava, S. (1999). The Big-Five trait taxonomy: History, measurement, and theoretical perspectives. In L.A. Pervin and O. P. John (Eds.). *Handbook of personality: Theory and research* (Vol. 2, pp. 102–138). New York: Guilford Press.

Jonason, P., Baughman, H., Carter, G., and Parker, P. (2015). Dorian Gray without his portrait: Psychological, social, and physical health costs associated with the Dark Triad. *Personality and Individual Differences, 78*, 5–13.

Jonason, P., Kavanagh, P., Webster, G., and Fitzgerald, D. (2011). Comparing the measured and latent Dark Triad: Are three measures better than one? *Journal of Methods and Measured in the Social Sciences, 2*(1), 28–44.

Jonason, P., Webster, G., Schmitt, D., Li, N., and Crysel, L. (2012). The antihero in popular culture: A life history theory of the Dark Triad. *Review of General Psychology, 16*(2), 192–199.

Jones, D. N., and Paulhus, D. L. (2011). The role of impulsivity in the Dark Triad of personality. *Personality and Individual Differences*, 51, 679–682.

Kazanjian, H. (Producer), and Marquand, R. (Director). (1983). *Star Wars: Return of the Jedi* [Motion Picture]. United States: 20th Century Fox.

Kennedy, K., Shearmur, A., Emanuel, S. (Producers), and Edwards, G. (Director). (2016). *Rogue One* [Motion Picture]. United States: Walt Disney Studios.

Kinberg, S., Reynolds, R., Donner, L. (Producers), and Miller, T. (Director). (2016). *Deadpool* [Motion Picture]. United States: 20th Century Fox.

Kurtz, G. (Producer), and Kershner, I. (Director). (1980). *Star Wars: The Empire Strikes Back* [Motion Picture]. United States: 20th Century Fox.

Kurtz, G. (Producer), and Lucas, G. (Director). (1977). *Star Wars: A New Hope* [Motion Picture]. United States: 20th Century Fox.

McCrae, R. R., and John, O. (1992). An introduction to the five-factor model and its applications. *Journal of Personality, 60*(2), 175–215.

Nolan, C. (Producer and Director), Thomas, E., and Roven, C. (Producers). (2008). *The Dark Knight* [Motion Picture]. United States: Warner Bros. Pictures.

Paulhus, D. L,. Neumann, C. S., and Hare, R. D. (2009). *Manual for the Hare Self-Report Psychopathy scale*. Toronto, Ontario, Canada: Multi-Health Systems.

Paulhus, D., and Williams, K. (2002). The Dark Triad of personality: Narcissism, Machiavellianism, and psychopathy. *Journal of Research in Personality, 36*, 556–563.

Qualtrics software, Version XM of Qualtrics. Copyright © 2018 Qualtrics. Qualtrics and all other Qualtrics product or service names are registered trademarks or trademarks of Qualtrics, Provo, UT, USA. (http://www.qualtrics.com).

Raskin, R., and Hall, C. S. (1981). The Narcissistic Personality Inventory: Alternate form reliability and further evidence of construct validity. *Journal of Personality Assessment, 45*(2), 159–162.

Rosenthal, S., Montoya, R., Ridings, L., Rieck, S. and Hooley, J., (2011). Further evidence of the Narcissistic Personality Inventory's validity problems: A meta-analytic investigation—Response to Miller, Maples, and Campbell (this issue). *Journal of Research in Personality, 45*(5), 408–416.

Roven, C., Suckle, R. (Producers), and Ayer, D. (Director). (2016). *Suicide Squad* [Motion Picture]. United States: Warner Bros. Pictures.

Watson, P., and Biderman, M. (1993). Narcissistic personality inventory factors, splitting and self-consciousness. *Journal of Personality Assessment, 61*(1), 41–57.

Yetişer, B. (2014). Do all roads lead to Rome? The moderating role of culture and age in predicting construal level on Machiavellianism. *Journal of Yasar University, 9*(36), 6261–6380.

Chapter Four

The New Definition of Good and Bad Guys in the Context of Psychology, World Beliefs, and Politics

Narcissism, trolls, and rivalries were the buzzwords of 2016 just as much as our villain and antihero theme. It was an election year. An election year that took the media world by storm. While the big screens the world over show-cased battles between heroes, villains, and everything in between, the small screens nationwide were ablaze with a battle of a different nature in the form of political debates. The 2016 election had begun to heat up and created an uproar. Name calling and nicknames were quickly flying in every direction. Many had hailed Trump as the "Troll in Chief" and a narcissist, including former opponent Ted Cruz (as cited in Wright, Kopan, and Manchester, 2016). At the same time, Trump's camp threw out the "Crooked Hillary" rant in full force via Twitter (realDonaldTrump, 2016). We can see this even now with Trump still using his Twitter handle to call out his newest opponent, "Sleepy Joe" for the 2020 election round (realDonaldTrump, March 2, 2020). Americans were fighting back and forth over ideology and beliefs across the battlefield of Twitter, trying to pick the candidate who maybe held the same ones they did. Or at least claimed to. Rivalries and belief systems were brought to the main stage through all of this, just as it continues to be with election campaigns since.

Similarly, popular culture rivalries came to light that year. *DC Universe* characters Batman and Superman came face to face to duke it out in the rain March of 2016. The Kryptonite-laced and armored fight divided fans much the same as the political debates all the way up until Bruce discovered Clark's mother's name (oh, the great Martha discussion) (Roven, Snyder, and Snyder, 2016). Two months later fans were proclaiming themselves to be "Team Iron Man" or "Team Captain America" as Marvel's *Civil War* hit theaters (Feige, Russo, and Russo, 2016). These films, along with others, recreated a trend of identifying your "team" and arguing for said team's merit over another. Just as the politicians argued and called out names at each other, fans and stans alike stood their ground over their teams via Twitter and Tumblr posts.

This trend brought us to the idea of delving into these beliefs, both popular culture beliefs (i.e., Team Iron Man vs. Team Captain America, Justice League vs. the Avengers, Jedi vs. Sith, etc.) and broader political and world beliefs. Research related to cultivation theory has long stated that media, be it the nightly news, the latest superhero film, or a disgruntled tweet, has the power to shape perceptions of the audience (Nan, 2011). Media has the power to act as a socialization agent, providing information and acting as a model for behaviors for viewers; this in turn can have a very persuasive impact (Shrum, 1999). Which can be of importance, as we know Hollywood is not one to stay silent on political ideas or world beliefs, no matter the side.

Be it Mark Ruffalo announcing an endorsement for Bernie Sander's 2020 campaign (MarkRuffalo, 2019) or the character the man plays arguing with Tony Stark on the topic of world safety in 2015 (Feige and Whedon), politics and popular culture can go hand in hand. Popular culture, especially film, has the potential to be political in a number of ways, both implicit and explicit. For every *Colbert Report* (Stewart, Purcell, and Colbert, 2014) there is a *Star Wars* film commenting on power and division (Kurtz and Lucas, 1977). Some films will highlight a very distinct opinion and ideology, while others may be acting as propaganda by leaving out one side of the argument, and some are purely historical and showcase specific events in time (Yenerall, 2013).

This, of course, was nothing new, nor did it start with the rise of *Star Wars* and Comedy Network's commentary. Film has provided commentary on politics nearly since its inception. Charles Chaplin graced screens in 1940 as Hynkel, a satirical response to Adolf Hitler and his growing power. Americans hadn't even entered World War II at the time this movie, *The Great Dictator,* entered movie theaters across the country. Now, nearly 80 years later, we have Taika Waititi, famed director of *Thor: Ragnarok,* doing the same thing with his successful film *Jojo Rabbit* (2019). In an interview, Waititi stated:

> Comedy for me is a really important tool... "It really irks me that it gets overlooked so often as a meaningful form of art because throughout history comedy has been, I think, the strongest weapon in commenting on society and issues. And dictators, kings and royalty, they hate being made fun of. You know, when people make jokes about them, it drives them bananas. (as cited in Buddenhage, 2020)

The films showcasing rivalries were doing very similar things to these purely satirical, politically driven movies. To some degree or another, many of the popular superhero and science fiction films referenced above for 2016 were providing subtle commentary on world views and politics. In fact, it has possibly become even more obvious, thanks to our political figures. Although this occurred after our study, many fans of the Avengers were appalled to see a Trump campaign account tweet out the now famous video of his face superimposed over the villainous Thanos's (*Marvel Universe*). Trump smiles, just as the villain himself does, before recreating the "snap," dusting the politicians behind the 2019 impeachment inquiry and announcing how his re-election was "inevitable" (TrumpWarRoom, 2019). The political world turned to the fictional then and has continued to do so. With the 2020 election campaign, Trump's campaign manager boasted about the "Death Star" from *Star Wars* lore that they have been building over the years against the Democrats (Parscale, 2020). We then see the return of the Avengers theme with Stephen Colbert clapping back at Trump's Thanos with his own parody in response to the Republican National Convention that same year (Drum, 2020). Star Wars, Avengers . . . all being used in discussing our political ideologies and information.

This marked a shift from the comic books commenting on the political atmosphere to the politicians utilizing the comics to shape their own commentary and to fit their agendas. The former has been active for decades, but the latter felt different. We have seen our favorite superheroes speak out on global issues and meet political or historical figures. We have seen Captain America punch out Hitler (Simon and Kirby, 1941). Spider-Man (*Marvel Universe*) saved President Obama's inauguration day (Waid, Jimenez, Wells, and Nuck, 2009). Even Deadpool (*Marvel Universe*) rescues a civilian by taking her to see the now infamous play on Alexander Hamilton (Duggan, Lolli, and Moore, 2016).

Due to all of this, we began diving into how we would approach world beliefs and views as psychologists and researchers. We knew that we did not want to solely look at Republican versus Democratic ideals and affiliations as the world of politics seemed to be changing with the appearance, and eventual success, of Donald Trump. In the new political sphere, we found ourselves in what felt like something more. Democrat, Republican, Conservative, Liberal . . . all these words began to take on different meanings and representations. Our search ultimately brought us to research on social dominance orientation and right-wing authoritarianism.

Social dominance orientation (SDO) revolves around beliefs related to and surrounding in-groups and out-groups; more specifically, the desire one has for their in-group to have higher status and power over the perceived out-group. This theory largely explores the social hierarchy involved and beliefs related to inequality in society as a result of the social order. It is believed that this allows groups to create consensus around views and rankings between groups, thus minimizing conflicts and normalizing oppression of the out-group. As a result, Pratto, Sidanius, Stallworth, and Malle found that stronger SDO is correlated with beliefs such as sexism, conservatism, and patriotism (1994). They also found it to be related to beliefs that could indicate opposition to equal rights for lesbian, gay, bisexual, transgender, queer or questioning, intersex, asexual and/or allied (LGBTQIA+) individuals, people of color, and women. While these views are not explicitly linked to the views of the Republican Party per its definition, this same study demonstrated that individuals strong in SDO were more likely to identify as a member of that political party in the United States as well.

Right-wing authoritarianism (RWA), though similar in nature to SDO, offered more information and was rooted in much history. Since the rise of fascism in the 1930s, people have been researching and looking to explain what was first viewed as an authoritarian personality. Essentially, researchers wanted to know why people were willing to submit to authority figures such as Hitler (Altemeyer, 1998). This has since morphed into RWA, which encompasses views related to traditionalism and conservatism. Those who possess high RWA typically uphold the values and mission of established social norms, have a tendency to submit to the perceived authority figure, and have a more black-and-white view of the world comparatively (Benjamin, 2014). Individuals tend to view the world as a dangerous place and, therefore, act accordingly (Duckitt, 2015).

Although these each can reflect and be correlated to views of political parties, they both speak to broader societal views and actions of those who hold these views. Both theories have been correlated to themes of prejudice and discrimination and, to an extent, hostility toward whoever the perceived outgroup of the week is (Whitley, 1999). This felt particularly relevant at the time we began this study. Many were clouting Trump not only as the "troll in chief" and the "narcissist" previously mentioned, but also as something more. A conversation around potential prejudice and racism had been sparked with his speeches and tweets. He created talking points leading up to the election over immigration and the infamous wall he promised to build.

Trump's "Make America Great Again" (MAGA) slogan was partially rooted in his commentary around Mexican immigration bringing in crime and drugs, and the supposed fall of the American way (Huber, 2016). The initial outcry gave way to supporters soon screaming the slogan at rallies, wearing MAGA merchandise, and ultimately aligning with his policies that held what many viewed as discriminatory language and attitudes toward Latinos. It was becoming more and more obvious as the election day approached that Americans were not as progressive in regard to prejudices as many had believed and hoped, and it cemented the idea that things were more than just Republican versus Democrat for this election year, and sadly in many ways since.

We are writing this as conversations around race, privilege, and discrimination have once again been sparked. People have died due to hate. George Floyd has died. Ahmaud Arbery as well. And Breonna Taylor. Others could unfortunately be included in this list, and it has likely grown since the time of us writing this. Days after George Floyd's death brought about protests of those just trying to highlight the sadness, the anger, the horrid nature of all of this, the President of the United States, the same country built on a history of protests, called those taking action "thugs" and incited violence through Twitter (realDonaldTrump, May 29, 2020).

When this tweet was sent out, Twitter acted, flagging it as "glorifying violence" as part of a new "fact checking" campaign. This same campaign has incited Trump and his supporters to lash out in a more "authoritarian" way through executive orders and retaliations (Lutz, 2020). Furthermore, it is not just confined to the world of Twitter. As 2020 continued, we saw Trump sending out armed forces to various cities to quell peaceful protests about perceived racial injustices that he deemed "riots" (Shannon, 2020). This brings up an interesting point. In fact, many have argued that one's views of authoritarianism largely influences political party selection, with those who possess more authoritarian traits or beliefs aligning with the Republican Party. Researchers argue that this has created the polarization we have been seeing in political parties and brought stronger desire to vote with your party no matter the issue or candidate (Dunwoody and Plane, 2019). Recent studies have taken this a step further and found that authoritarianism as a broad concept and belief influenced the support behind Donald Trump (MacWilliams, 2016). Dunwoody and Plane replicated this study in 2019, utilizing a specific measure of RWA to find the same results. Authoritarian views appeared to be more important at this time than simply asking if one was a Democrat or Republican in the current political climate.

Additionally, it has been found that political interest and knowledge is related to personality traits. As we discussed in previous chapters, we had already begun to utilize the Big Five and Dark Triad in our research. These same measures and traits have been utilized in studies on political interest. Openness (see previous chapters for definitions) has been linked to a desire to gain political knowledge and participate in politics at a local and national level. Extraversion has also been shown to indicate a greater likelihood of political participation at the local level. Emotional stability (formerly neuroticism), furthermore, has evidence for being a strong indicator for political interest and knowledge (Gerber, Huber, Doherty, and Dowling, 2011).

Moreover, we could not neglect the significance of words such as "troll" and "narcissism" that were being tossed about on various media in 2016. Narcissism, as previously discussed, is one part/trait of the Dark Triad. Research around all three of the Dark Triad traits has been linked to a higher likelihood to engage in Internet trolling behaviors. These behaviors include purposely posting upsetting comments and responses to others, deceiving online users, spamming, and more (Buckels, Trapnell, and Paulhus, 2014). Trolls have traditionally been viewed as despicable and hateful individuals, yet many were supporting a potential "troll in chief" as he began to inch closer to Clinton in the polls that summer. It is important to note that we are discussing the relationship between trolling and the Dark Triad in this study. We aren't measuring Internet trolling separately with its own measure in this study, but we do begin to measure and discuss it in more detail in chapter 6.

With all this information, we began to speculate on how to craft this study. We looked to the movies hitting the screens and the "teams" people were choosing to align with. In doing so, we decided to pit the Avengers against the Justice League, the Sith against the Jedi, and everything in between. We constructed a list of popular Marvel, DC, and Star Wars characters to use alongside personality, SDO, and RWA measures. Furthermore, we ensured that our characters were diverse in terms of race, gender, and ideology.

Previous researchers had created and utilized measures for the SDO, including the 16-item Social Dominance Orientation Scale (Pratto, Sidanius, Stallworth, and Malle, 1994). This measure utilizes the items to highlight views on equality through social, moral, and economic statements. The degree to which one agrees with each statement indicates a higher or lower SDO. Authoritarianism research largely uses the RWA Scale in a variety of forms. The short form (Altemeyer, 1998), a 32-item inventory, has been found as a valid measure of these views (Rattazzi, Bobbio, and Canova, 2007).

These measures rounded out our study. All participants were presented with both of these measures (the RWA and the SDO) along with the Big Five Inventory (John and Srivastava, 1999) that we started using in chapter 1, and each of the three components of the Dark Triad first measured in chapter 3. Machiavellianism was measured by the MACH-IV (Yetişer, 2014), psychopathy was measured by the SRP-III (Paulhus, Neumann, and Hare, 2009), and narcissism was measured by the NPI (Raskin and Hall, 1981), demographics (see appendix A), and 450 plus characters (see appendix B) via Qualtrics (http://www.qualtrics.com) (Qualtrics, Provo, UT). As usual, participants went through the list and rated each character on a scale of one to seven as to the degree to which they "liked" the characters (1 = Strongly dislike while 7 = Strongly like). For every Luke Skywalker we wanted his Darth Vader, and we payed attention to "teams" of characters (Star Wars versus Star Trek,

Marvel versus DC, etc.). We did allow for individuals to skip (and not rate) characters that they did not know. This prevented characters and teams from being skewed by lesser known members.

There was a total of 404 participants. Sixty-one percent of respondents identified as fans of superhero-related genres and video games. Thirty-seven percent identified as a fan of Marvel, seven percent identified as fans of DC, 31 percent identified as a fan of both Marvel and DC while 23 percent identified as a fan of "neither." Perhaps most interestingly, 26 percent self-identified as Democrat, 34 percent self-identified as Republican, and 19 percent self-identified as Independent.

Furthermore, 398 of our 404 participants indicated the candidate whom they would most likely (or like) to vote for. Something that should be pointed out . . . we collected data before, during, and after the primaries as well as the general elections, and after Donald Trump's inauguration. In the lead, Bernie Sanders took 34.4 percent of the "votes" from our pool of participants. In second, we see Trump, himself, with 28 percent of our participants identifying as supporters. In third, we see Hillary Clinton with 14.4 percent. Marco Rubio with 7.7 percent, Ted Cruz with 7.2 percent, and John Kasich with 5 percent round out the top candidates for this study.

All analyses were completed examining all eight sub-components of personality along with the RWA and SDO scales. As always, a Bonferroni correction was conducted to counter the number of analyses conducted and to protect the Type I error rate; the significance level has been lowered from $p < .05$ to $p < .005$ to determine significance.

We were able to find some interesting team results. (These team results also created some interesting questions surrounding fandoms. Please see chapter 9 and appendix D for more information about our research into fandoms.) Of the 15 characters who were all predicted as being liked more based on higher agreeableness, nine of these are *Marvel Universe* characters (Ant Man, Beast, Black Widow, Captain America, Daredevil, Jubilee, Professor X, Spider-Man, and Winter Soldier) and five are *Star Wars* characters (Anakin Skywalker, Leia Organa*, Luke Skywalker, Obi-Wan Kenobi, and Yoda*).[1] Only one character was not a part of these two groups (Wonder Woman*, who is part of the *DC Universe*). A similar result was also found with narcissism. Lower narcissism scores predicted more liking of a total of six characters. All but one of these (Batman, who is part of the *DC Universe*) are part of the *Marvel Universe* (Hank Pym, Iron Man, Jessica Jones*, Rogue, and Wolverine).

Those individual characters associated with higher scores on the Social Dominance Orientation Scale (SDO) are all representatives from the *Marvel Universe*: Beast, Hawkeye, Punisher*, and War Machine*. Those characters associated with lower SDO scores are all representatives from *Star Wars*: Kylo Ren, Luke Skywalker, Palpatine, and Snoke. It is important to note that this dataset was collected before *The Rise of Skywalker* (Kennedy, Abrams, and Rejwan, 2019) when the storylines for both Kylo and Luke were not yet solidified.

One could make the argument that we have two groups represented within the *Marvel Universe* with some Marvel properties being controlled by Disney (Avengers) and others being controlled, at the time, by Fox (X-Men). While there are many crossovers between Marvel characters in the comics, these crossovers have been limited in film. The X-Men franchise (both comics and movies) have been used to tackle many issues since its arrival on the comics scene. "(T)he X-Men have changed vastly over the years, and this basis has given countless writers and artists the opportunity to tackle heavy subjects like classism, racism, homophobia, and ableism through mainstream comics" (Century, 2019, para. 1). It was then little surprise when a total of seven X-Men team members were predicted as more liked by lower RWA scores (fewer right-wing attitudes): Deadpool, Jean Grey, Magneto*, Mystique*, Nightcrawler*, Professor X, and Shadow Kat. The other characters on this list were all representatives of minorities: Black Panther (*Marvel Universe*), Finn (*Star Wars*), Luke Cage (*Marvel Universe*), and Mace Windu (*Star Wars*). With this, we see more characters of color, female identifying characters, and LGBTQIA+ characters associated with lower RWA scores. As with narcissism and agreeableness, all these characters are either from Marvel or Star Wars. Interestingly, the only character associated with higher levels of right-wing authoritarianism (RWA) was Superman.

The results highlight an interesting phenomenon where we see characters from groups traditionally viewed as minorities or oppressed in some way aligning with lower authoritarian and social dominance orientation, comparatively. Those who endorse liking those characters tend to align with views we would consider more "liberal" and inclusive. It also highlights characters that have been utilized in a political nature. X-Men characters, many of which we see in our results here, have been used as commentary on social issues since they were created. In the 1960s, when they were first introduced, writers behind the Marvel characters used the stories and "mutant" genes as commentary against racial prejudice and discrimination. It aligned with the times. Just as the Bryan Singer movies in the 2000s highlighted issues related to homophobia and equality. And the recent iterations of *First Class* and its sequel speak on religious freedom and discrimination related to Jewish faith and Nazism (Parks and Hughey, 2017).

Characters have meaning. Be it X-Men combatting heavy political topics or personal stories we have with these characters. For this reason, representation and diversity in these characters matter. We see ourselves in our characters and in the stories we love. They are important in various ways and context. It also raises an important question . . . besides politics and individual preference, what other things influence our love for characters . . . or love in general? And what about love for our favorite couples (more on that in chapter 5)? This study taught us a lot. It illustrates how beliefs and current events likely influence our love of characters. It left us wanting to know more, and more curious about love in general.

NOTE

1. The asterisk denotes characters who were only marginally significant. They met the $p < .05$ benchmark but not the $p < .005$ benchmark.

REFERENCES

Altemeyer, B. (1998). The other "authoritarian personality." *Advances in Experimental Social Psychology, 30,* 47–92.

Benjamin Jr., A. (2014). Chasing the elusive left-wing authoritarian: An examination of Altemeyer's right-wing authoritarianism and left-wing authoritarianism scales. *National Social Science Journal, 43,* 7–13.

Buckels, E., Trapnell, P., and Paulhus, D. (2014). Trolls just want to have fun. *Personality and Individual Differences, 67,* 97–102.

Buddenhage, R. (2020, February 2). Jojo Rabbit writer-director Taika Waititi: Comedy is a powerful weapon against dictators. CBS News retrieved from https://www.cbsnews .com/news/jojo-rabbit-writer-director-taika-waititi-comedy-is-a-powerful-weapon -against-dictators/?ftag=CNM-00-10aab6i&linkId=81620053&fbclid=IwAR0eD A24UpzMyTO9_ZKg1-3Lq1ZUXEPxTGYQS79j3eJk1XLbNFlamX0OseM.

Century, S. (June 7, 2019). *X-Men as a Queer Metaphor.* SyFy Wire. Retrieved from https://www.syfy.com/syfywire/x-men-as-a-queer-metaphor.

Chaplin, C. (Producer and Director). 1940. *The Great Dictator* [Motion Picture]. United States: Charles Chaplin Film Corporation.

Drum, N. (2020, Aug 25). Stephen Colbert releases new Avengers: Endgame parody of Republican National Convention. Retrieved from https://comicbook.com/mar vel/news/avengers-endgame-stephen-colbert-parody-rnc/.

Duckitt, J. (2015). Authoritarian personality. *International Encyclopedia of the Social & Behavioral Sciences, 2nd edition, vol. 2* Oxford: Elsevier.

Duggan, G., Lolli, M., and Moore, T. (2016). *Deadpool No. 20.* New York, New York: Marvel Comics.

Dunwoody, P., and Plane, D. (2019). The influence of authoritarianism and outgroup threat on political affiliations and support for antidemocratic policies. *Peace and Conflict: Journal of Peace Psychology, 25*(3), 198–210.

Feige, K. (Producer), Russo, A., and Russo, J. (Directors). (2016). *Captain America: Civil War* [Motion Picture]. United States: Walt Disney Studios.

Feige, K. (Producer), and Whedon, J. (Director). (2015). *Avengers: Age of Ultron* [Motion Picture]. United States: Walt Disney Studios.

Gerber, A., Huber, G., Doherty, D., and Dowling, C. (2011). Personality traits and the consumption of political information. *American Politics Research, 39*(1), 32–84.

Huber, L. (2016). "Make America great again!": Donald Trump, racist nativism, and the virulent adherence to white supremacy amid U.S. demographic change. *Charleston Law Review, 10,* 215–248.

John, O. P, and Srivastava, S. (1999). The Big-Five trait taxonomy: History, measurement, and theoretical perspectives. In L.A. Pervin and O. P. John (Eds.). *Handbook of personality: Theory and research* (Vol. 2, pp. 102–138). New York: Guilford Press.

Kennedy, K., Abrams, J. J., and Rejwan, M. (Producers). (2019). *Star Wars: The Rise of Skywalker* [Motion Picture]. United States: Walt Disney Studios.

Kurtz, G. (Producer) and Lucas, G. (Director). (1977). *Star Wars: A New Hope* [Motion Picture]. United States: 20th Century Fox.

Lutz, E. (2020, May 28). Trump, infuriated by Twitter's fact check, goes full authoritarian. *Vanity Fair*. Retrieved from: https://www.vanityfair.com/news/2020/05/trump-infuriated-by-twitter-fact-check-goes-full-authoritarian-executive-order.

MacWilliams, M. (2016). Who decides when the party doesn't? Authoritarian voters and the rise of Donald Trump. *PS: Political Science and Politics, 49*(4), 716–721.

MarkRuffalo (2019, December 6). ICYMI: I'm proud to endorse @BernieSanders for the 2020 Presidential Election [Tweet]. https://twitter.com/MarkRuffalo/status/1202955237146923008.

Nan, X. (2011). Influence of television on viewing and sensation seeking on adolescents' unrealistic perceptions about smoking and smokers: Evidence from a national survey. *Mass Communication and Society, 14,* 643–665.

Parks, G., and Hughey, M. (2017). A choice of weapons: The X-Men and the metaphor for approaches to racial equality. *The Supplement, 92*(5), 1–26. Retrieved from https://www.repository.law.indiana.edu/cgi/viewcontent.cgi?article=11267&context=ilj.

Parscale, B. (2020, May 7). For nearly three years we have been building a juggernaut campaign (Death Star). It is firing on all cylinders. Data, Digital, TV, Political, Surrogates, Coalitions, etc. In a few days we start pressing FIRE for the first time [Tweet]. https://twitter.com/parscale/status/1258388669544759296?s=20.

Paulhus, D. L., Neumann, C. S., and Hare, R. D. (2009). *Manual for the Self-Report Psychopathy scale.* Toronto: Multi-Health Systems.

Pratto, F., Sidanius, J., Stallworth, L., and Malle, B. (1994). Social dominance orientation: A personality variable predicting social and political attitudes. *Journal of Personality and Social Psychology, 67*(4), 741–763.

Qualtrics software, Version XM of Qualtrics. Copyright © 2018 Qualtrics. Qualtrics and all other Qualtrics product or service names are registered trademarks or trademarks of Qualtrics, Provo, UT, USA. (http://www.qualtrics.com).

Raskin, R. N., and Hall, C. S. (1981). The Narcissistic Personality Inventory: Alternative form reliability and further evidence of construct validity. *Journal of Personality Assessment, 45,* 159–160.

Rattazzi, A., Bobbio, A., and Canova, L. (2007). A short version of the Right-Wing Authoritarianism (RWA) Scale. *Personality and Individual Differences, 43,* 1223–1234.

realDonaldTrump (2020, May 29). These THUGS are dishonoring the memory of George Floyd, and I won't let that happen. Just spoke to Governor Tim Walz and told him that the Military is with him all the way. Any difficulty and we will assume control but, when the looting starts, the shooting starts. Thank you! [Tweet]. https://twitter.com/realDonaldTrump/status/1266231100780744704.

realDonaldTrump (2020, March 2). WOW! Sleep Joe doesn't know where he is or what he's doing. Honestly I don't think he even knows what office he's running for! [Tweet]. https://twitter.com/realDonaldTrump/status/1234695977656881154.

realDonaldTrump (2016, April 17). Crooked Hillary Clinton is spending a fortune on ads against me. I am the one person she doesn't want to run against. Will be such fun! [Tweet]. https://twitter.com/realDonaldTrump/status/721695114943442946?ref_src=twsrc%5Etfw%7Ctwcamp%5Etweetembed%7Ctwterm%5E721695114943442946&ref_url=https%3A%2F%2Fwww.washingtonexaminer.com%2F2016-in-tweets-from-donald-trump.

Roven, C., Snyder, D. (Producers), and Snyder, Z. (Director). (2016). *Batman v. Superman: Dawn of Justice* [Motion Picture]. United States: Warner Bros. Pictures.

Shannon, J. (2020, July 25). Live updates from weekend protests: Man shot to death in Austin, Seattle police declare riot, armed militia in Louisville. USA Today. Retrieved from https://www.usatoday.com/story/news/nation/2020/07/25/protest-live-blog-portland-chicago-nyc-louisville-updates/5501660002/.

Shrum, L. J. (1999). Television and persuasion: Effects of the programs between the ads. *Psychology & Marketing, 16*(2), 119–140.

Simon, J., and Kirby, J. (1941). *Captain America comics No. 1.* New York, New York: Marvel Comics.

Stewart, J., Purcell, T., and Colbert, S. (Producers). (2014). *Colbert Report* [Television Series]. New York, NY: Spartina Productions.

TrumpWarRoom (2019, December 10). House Democrats can push their sham impeachment all they want. President Trump's re-election is inevitable [Tweet]. https://twitter.com/TrumpWarRoom/status/1204503645607333888.

Waid, M., Jimenez, P., Wells, Z., and Nuck, T. (2009). *The amazing Spider-Man No. 583.* New York, New York: Marvel Comics.

Waititi, T. (Producer and Director). (2019). *Jojo Rabbit* [Motion Picture]. United States: Fox Searchlight.

Whitley, B. (1999). Right-wing authoritarianism, social dominance orientation, and prejudice. *Journal of Personality and Social Psychology, 77*(1), 126–134.

Wright, D., Kopan, T., and Manchester, J. (2016, May 3). Cruz unloads with epic takedown of 'pathological liar,' 'narcissist' Donald Trump. CNN. Retrieved from https://www.cnn.com/2016/05/03/politics/donald-trump-rafael-cruz-indiana/index.html.

Yenerall, K. (2013). Politics and pop culture: Citizenship, satire, and social change. *Juniata Voices,* 93–106.

Yetişer, B. (2014). Do all roads lead to Rome? The moderating role of culture and age in predicting construal level on Machiavellianism. *Journal of Yasar University, 9*(36), 6328–6337.

Chapter Five

Love Is Love

Team Iron Man versus Team Captain America (*Marvel Universe*), along with all the other rivalries mentioned in the previous chapter, were not the first time people fought for their "team." In fact, eight years prior to these films, a very different debate divided fans. The "shipping wars" had started and fans the world over had chosen their sides . . . you were either Team Edward or Team Jacob (*Twilight*). While Stephanie Meyers' *Twilight* series (2006) has since died down in popularity, you couldn't walk into the local mall without seeing racks lined with shirts proclaiming your "team," your choice for love-sick Bella Swan.

It has been said that all is fair in love and war, and those two things definitely go together with fandom. Fans have fought for their favorite couples for decades. Long before the love triangle of *Twilight*, there was the love triangle and "who will she choose" around Buffy, Angel, and Spike (Whedon, 1997 [*Buffy the Vampire Slayer*]). Fans chose their "ship," their couple they wanted to see come together and stay together on screen. It seems as if fans almost naturally fantasize about or imagine their characters together in various intimate ways, especially when the shows or books themselves aren't delivering. For this reason, fans have been "shipping" in fan media, be it fanfiction or otherwise, for decades.

Furthermore, fans get to create relationships with diversity, something that has not always found its way to the screens of Hollywood. With shipping, people express their love for same-sex couples, mixed-race couples, mixed species, and more. People can ship "slash" couples, meaning romantic partners of the same sex. This allows for LGBTQIA+ representation that has often been lacking in popular culture. In fact, this dates back to shippers first writing slash fanfiction of Kirk/Spock (*Star Trek*) for a fan magazine in the 1970s

(Hale-Stern, 2018). Since, Tumblr, Archive of Our Own, and so many more fan havens have embraced shipping and love of all shapes, sizes, and forms.

This is in stark contrast to what we see at times in popular culture. With many highlighting problems in Hollywood for excluding marginalized groups or creating stories that are not reflective of realistic experiences, diversity and representation have become a much-discussed topic. The topic continues, be it the #OscarsSoWhite tag speaking out against a lack of diversity in the famed award show in 2016 or the all-male line-up for the "Best Director" category of the same show not even four years later. It continues to be a problem.

And it matters. Former First Lady Michelle Obama said it well when she stated, "For so many people, television and movies may be the only way they understand people who aren't like them" (as cited in Jones, 2016, para. 1). This could explain why we see fans change it up with their fanfiction and art, depicting characters in "ships" that they would not always see on their mainstream media. Things may have changed a great deal since the 1970s, but it has been slow. Programs such as *Will and Grace, Glee,* and *Schitt's Creek,* all of which were considered innovative when they first aired, still continue to be a newer phenomenon. Disney has even announced its first bisexual lead in the form of fourteen-year-old Luz of the animated series *The Owl House* (Variety, 2020). These programs are still gaining attention. But they have brought about a change, and a lot of love for them.

Because, love is . . . well, love is love, of course. But is that true? We love our pets, we love our friends, we love our partners, we love our phones, we love our children, and sometimes we love each other. But is the love that we feel for our friends really the same as the love that we feel for our children? All in all, there seems to be quite a lot of debate about what love is and exactly how it is measured. So . . . what is love?

Just like personality, a single definition of love is difficult to pin down, with many sources even disagreeing on the types of love associated with ancient Greece. The number can range from as few as five to as many as eight, and it is not uncommon to see love boiled down to as few as two (see Hatfield and Rapson, 1993, for their discussion on companionate versus passionate love). According to Lee (1973) there are six types of love: Eros, Ludus/Ludos, Storge, Pragma, Mania, and Agape. These types were derived from Guttman-Lingoes Smallest Space Analysis procedure (see Lee, 1977) which is much like the factor analyses that were used to derive the Big Five personality traits first discussed in chapter 1.

The first type of love is Eros, which is what we typically think of as romantic love. This is the kind of love that we usually associate with love for a partner. Ludus (sometimes referenced as Ludos) is love built around conquest, or game playing. In the age of social media and Tinder, this is now often associated with the stereotypical "player" or "fuckboy." Storge is love built on friendship. This can be thought of as either the love that we have for a friend, or the love for a partner that is first built upon by friendship. Pragma is love that is built upon practicality. Often, arranged marriages and courtships are framed as a practical love. Mania is associated with obsession, possession, and passion. This type of love is often discussed in terms of dependence or "fatal attraction." It is a love where the players are usually on uneven footing. Agape can be thought of as the opposite of Mania. It is a love characterized by selflessness. This is usually the way that love between mother and child is characterized.

Each of these types of love can be found in various fandoms from all types of popular culture. The relationship between Edward and Bella in *Twilight* captured the hearts of "Twihards" as the shining example of Eros, and a love that would almost literally last forever. The death of Lily Potter (*Harry Potter*) to save her beloved son Harry is the ultimate example of Agape: A love so strong and powerful as to defy the curse of death, itself. The love between Frodo Baggins and Samwise Gamgee (*LOTR*) is the force that leads to the ultimate destruction of the "ring to rule them all" and the defeat of the dark.

People may experience different love styles in their lives, just as one may prefer one ship over another in popular culture. So, what does our shipping preferences say about our love preferences? What is it that we are (you are) shipping? Are we looking for the romance, the friendship, or the passion? And, perhaps even more importantly, are there any differences in love itself?

The first thing that we did was to select a measure of love that matched our operational definition. We first chose the 42-item relationship-specific version of the Hendrick and Hendrick Love Attitudes Scale (LAS) (Hendrick and Hendrick, 1990). This scale is based directly on the work, and the six-component definition of love, as presented by Lee (1973). It has been shown to have good psychometric properties and has been used in several studies (Hendrick and Hendrick, 1990). We quickly realized that total survey length was problematic when we began construction on our shipping list. Ultimately, the Love Attitudes Scale was the direction that we wanted to pursue, so we opted for the 24-item (four-item subscales) Love Attitudes Scale: Short Form (LAS: SF). Associated data with the short form have demonstrated stronger psychometric properties than the previous 42-item measure (Hendrick, Hendrick, and Dicke, 1998).

We then added our standard set of demographic questions (see appendix A). These questions covered basic information about participants (gender, sexual orientation, education, etc.), but they also included a little more detailed information about sexual orientation. Finally, we constructed our list of ships (see appendix B for some examples of these). We gathered these from fanfiction sites, Tumblr, Reddit, blogs, and our own personal ships. These ships ultimately crossed almost every genre of the nerddom (comics, movie, TV, books, anime, etc.). The first of these lists were gathered and generated in 2018 and contained a total of 195 ships. The second list updated the first list to now include a total of 256 ships in popular culture offerings released through December 2019.

We distributed our survey via Qualtrics (http://www.qualtrics.com) (Qualtrics, Provo, UT); but in addition to our usual venues, we also started soliciting from our own social media accounts. One of the problems that we have had with national and convenience samples is that a certain percentage of our population (a rather significantly large percentage of our population) are not at all familiar with pop culture. Since one of the members of this writing trio had no idea what "ships" and "One True Parings" (OTPs) even were before we started this project, we were afraid that we would not be able to get a large enough sample of individuals familiar with ships to get a usable dataset. So, we did what all good researchers have started doing . . . we turned to Tumblr, Twitter, and Facebook for a little data collection assistance (in addition to our usual venues).

Once the survey was constructed and distributed, it followed our usual style. Participants gave consent to the study and the conditions and were asked to complete demographic questions. Once these sections were completed, participants completed the 24-item LAS: SF (2018 through 2020 versions) and, for the 2020 version only, the nine-item Fan Identity Scale (Vinney, Dill-Shackleford, Plante, and Bartsch, 2019) (see chapters 9 and 10 for more information about this). Once these were completed, participants were presented with either the 195 (2018) or the 256 (2020) list of selected ships. The characters ranged from comic books to literature to film and television. The characters represented a variety of genres, including superhero media, science fiction, fantasy, and anime from a breadth of outlets, publishers, and production companies. They were randomized, rather than categorized into specific genres or media. Participants responded with the level to which they "like" each ship on a scale of one to seven. A score of one indicated that the participant strongly disliked a ship. A score of seven indicated that they strongly liked the named ship. For unknown ships, participants could mark "does not know" so that a lack of knowledge of a ship would not influence the results.

Scales and items were scored in both 2018 and 2020. The initial dataset included 823 participants, and the 2020 dataset included results from a total of 1200 participants. As always with our research, all results remain anonymous and nothing can be linked back to any one participant. We also utilized manipulation checks to ensure that participants read items. The dataset was cleaned using two standard deviations along with the manipulation checks to be sure that participant data was usable and any data points that did not meet criteria were removed. Finally, any participant who had not completed at least 30 percent of the survey (they had completed questions on the LAS: SF and had attempted at least one ship) was removed from analyses.

We hypothesized that love is love, and that we would see few (if any) difference(s) between the types of love. We tested this with a MANOVA, most recently in January 2020. Additionally, we thought that ships would predict the type(s) of love that they were most associated with. For example, we would expect a slash ship like Kirk/Spock to be predictive of Storge (love built on friendship) or Pragma (the practical component of finding love on a spaceship with a limited population from which to choose). We used regressions to see which ships predicted which types of love while also being sure to implement Bonferroni corrections.

While not every ship was significant nor represented, we did find some interesting results. Perhaps most notable was that in our 2018 sample our most highly rated LGBTQIA+ couple stood in slot 45 (Poison Ivy/Harley Quinn [*DC Universe*]), but in our 2020 sample the highest LGBTQIA+ couple sat firmly in slot four (Billy/Teddy [*Wiccan/Hulkling; Marvel Universe*]). The 2018 list, in order, included: Superman/Lois Lane (*DC Universe*), Han/Leia (*Star Wars*), Glenn/Maggie (*The Walking Dead*), Mike/Eleven (*Stranger Things*), Jon/Daenerys (*Game of Thrones*), Batman/Catwoman (*DC Universe*), Wolverine/Jean Grey (*Marvel Universe*), Iron Man/Pepper (*Marvel Universe*), Black Panther/Nakia (*Marvel Universe*), and Peeta/Katniss (*Hunger Games*). The 2020 list, in order, included: Jaime/Brienne (*Game of Thrones*), Fitz/Simmons (*Marvel Universe*), Billy/Teddy (*Marvel Universe*), Kirk/Bones (*Star Trek*), Han/Leia (*Star Wars*), Ladybug/Cat Noir (*Miraculous Ladybug*), Aaron/Eric (*The Walking Dead*), Elsie/Clementine (*Westworld*), Supergirl/Mon El (*DC Universe*), and Jon/Ygritte (*Game of Thrones*).

There were a total of three LGBTQIA+ couples in our top ten in this newest sample. These results seem to suggest the normalization of the "love is love" concept. To further test this hypothesis, we compared the scores across all six types of love between those individuals who identified as LGBTQIA+ and those who did not in both 2018 and again in 2020. In both cases, neither of the MANOVAs were statistically significant (2018: Wilk's Lambda (6, 371) = .974, p = .13) (2020 (includes fandom measures for chapter 9): Wilk's Lambda (9, 157) = 1.63, p = .111.). Love really is just love. Well, except if you are a hardcore Disney fan, then love is a little different. Based on a MANOVA examining Disney fans' attitudes score across dimensions of love and personality, Disney fans are significantly higher across four separate types of love (Wilk's Lambda (14, 250) = 3.696, p < .001).

- Eros (Disney Fan = 14.9 vs Not A Fan = 13.67)
- Storge (Disney Fan = 13.64 vs Not A Fan = 11.29)
- Pragma (Disney Fan = 10.88 vs Not A Fan = 9.49)
- Agape (Disney Fan = 13.99 vs Not A Fan = 12.12)

So, there are no significant differences in love based on self-identified sexual identity, but there are differences in love based on fandoms. Love is love, except if you're a Disney fan; and then you love a little more. The top *Disney* ships, in order, include: Simba/Nala, Tarzan/Jane, Cinderella/Prince Charming, Belle/Beast, Woody/Bo-Peep, Snow White/Prince, Tiana/Prince Naveen, Carl/Ellie, Ariel/Prince Eric, and Mike/Sulley. But more on that to come. As April likes to say, the Disney fandom ruins everything, so please see chapter 9 for a more complete discussion on Disney.

As with many of our studies, we learned a lot and found new questions. In this case a mix of curiosity and annoyance at Disney, as well as reflections on how people approach their love of characters, raised serious questions about the influence of love and personality on fandoms. It is not always easy to find the beauty and light, even in studies primarily dealing with love. Many of these ships received a significant backlash and a certain amount of hate from those completing our study. For every Jaime/Brienne shipper there was someone in the background expressing deep dislike for the Dumbledore/Newt (*Harry Potter/Fantastic Beasts*) ship. In fact, it was our most hated ship, and Harry Potter fandom ships represented a total of eight of our 20 most hated ships. Which brings us to the trolls . . .

REFERENCES

Hale-Stern, K. (2018). I can't stop thinking about the first published Kirk/Spock slash fanfiction. The Mary Sue. Retrieved from: https://www.themarysue.com/first-published-slash-fanfiction/.

Hatfield, E., and Rapson, R. (1993). *Love, sex, and intimacy: The psychology, biology, and history.* New York, NY: Harper Collins.

Hendrick, C., and Hendrick, S. S. (1990). A relationship-specific version of the Love Attitudes Scale. *Journal of Social Behavior and Personality, 5*, 239–254.

Hendrick, C., Hendrick, S. S., and Dicke, A. (1998). The Love Attitudes Scale: Short Form. *Journal of Social and Personal Relationships, 15*(2), 147–159.

Jones, N. (2016, August 23). Michelle Obama explains why representation in pop culture matters. Vulture. Retrieved from: https://www.vulture.com/2016/08/michelle-obama-on-why-tv-representation-matters.html.

Lee, J. A. (1973). *The colors of love: An exploration of the ways of loving.* Don Mills, Ontario: New Press.

Lee, J. A. (1977). A typology of styles of loving. *PSPR, 3*, 173–182.

Meyers, S. (2006). *The Twilight Saga: New Moon*. New York: Little Brown.

Qualtrics software, Version XM of Qualtrics. Copyright © 2018 Qualtrics. Qualtrics and all other Qualtrics product or service names are registered trademarks or trademarks of Qualtrics, Provo, UT, USA. (http://www.qualtrics.com).

Variety. (2020, Aug. 17). 'The Owl House' makes history with Disney's first bisexual lead character. NBC News. Retrieved from: https://www.nbcnews.com/feature/nbc-out/owl-house-makes-history-disney-s-first-bisexual-lead-character-n1236947?cid=sm_npd_nn_fb_ma.

Vinney, C., Dill-Shackleford, K. E., Plante, C. N., and Bartsch, A. (2019, March 21). Development and validation of a measure of popular media fan identity and its relationship to well-being. *Psychology of Popular Media Culture*. Advance online publication.

Whedon, J. (Producer). (1997). *Buffy the Vampire Slayer* [Television Series]. United States: 20th Century Fox.

Chapter Six

Internet Trolls and Internet Addiction

As we've seen, fans love to show their love, and the Internet has become a huge outlet for many to do just that. They flock to websites like Twitter, Tumblr, and Reddit to express their opinions and connect to like-minded fans. However, it is not always about the love. While many seek friendly conversations about their favorites, others seek to send out "flames" and spread hateful rhetoric. And some become too consumed with the virtual mediums the Internet has to offer.

Many of us rely on computer- or Internet-based communication as part of our work and social lives. It has greatly shifted the way we talk to others and has opened the doors for communication and interaction across time zones, oceans, and even languages. Virtual communication is one of the corner stones of the Internet. Since the beginning, we have sent emails, sought out chat groups, and more as a way to talk and discuss with others, both friends and strangers. It also provides an anonymity we do not always have in our daily "real" lives. For this reason, it can be easier to craft hateful messages or degrade others without consequences. Computer-based communication allows for people to post an idealized version of themselves, just as much as a more deceptive and possibly cruel version (Hardaker, 2010).

For this reason, the rise of Internet culture has given birth to the creatures famously known as *Internet trolls* and a swarm of other issues related to behaviors and usage of the Internet. Trolls come in many shapes, forms, and sizes across the different mediums. A "troll" can take the form of a bully calling out others via the safety of Twitter or a trickster weaving chaos through the threads of Reddit. An Internet Troll is someone who engages in harassment and other unsociable behaviors in the comment sections of blogs, forums, videos, and more, with the goal of provoking, angering, or disturbing others (Craker and March, 2016).

They have become the modern-day cyberbullies who run amok. Some remain anonymous, hiding behind vague usernames, and others proudly step into the limelight, as we have already discussed in chapter 4 with regard to political figures. They appear to be their own breed, with distinct personality traits. This was something that we became more and more curious about as we continued our research journey. For that reason, we turned our attention to the personality traits of those watching, commenting on, and scrolling through one of the most popular websites of our time: YouTube.

The popular video-sharing website has been active for over a decade and has evolved into a media mogul with its own celebrities, brand deals, and programming. What was once a format to upload your videos for friends to watch, has only grown in its nearly 15 years of service to include vlogs, production companies, and so much more. Much like our previous studies on superheroes and other arenas of popular culture, YouTube has a huge following and millions of fans logging in on a daily basis. Only, rather than catching up with the likes of Batman and Superman (*DC Universe*), they are tuning in to see what crazy stunts the Paul Brothers are performing and what Shane Dawson has to say (more on Shane Dawson and *cancel culture* later in the chapter).

YouTube has given way to popular channels and programming over the years with very devoted followings. Be it Mythical Beasts who wake up every day to watch Rhett and Link eat bull testicles or those watching Jeffree Star serve the tea to the makeup world, YouTube is its own fandom in a sense with conventions and communities conversing. It is also a breeding ground for trolls, both in terms of the content creators and the fans commenting on the videos.

Many have commented on specific YouTube creators as "trolls." This has made headlines quite frequently with Logan Paul, specifically. The oldest of the Paul Brothers has gone under fire at many points for trolling everyone from the "flat earthers" to his younger brother (more on him in a minute) to his whole fan base. Logan Paul posted a video announcing to his fans and the whole world that he believed the world was flat. He went on to attend conventions for those who believed in this, claiming he was serious about his belief. However, prior to going out on stage to discuss his views, he could not keep a straight face to interviewers and spent the time giggling through his supposed claims (Weiss, 2018).

This incident comes just two years after Logan Paul was under fire for posting a video that showed what appeared to be a dead man's body. Paul, who had been filming what was supposedly a "haunted" forest, came across what allegedly was the body of a man who had died by suicide. Fans were outraged at how Paul cracked jokes and acted disrespectfully in the video, which he ultimately took down due to the criticism ("Logan Paul," 2018). This incident in particular brought up a lot of concerns as it related to mental health and suicide, topics that should not be taken lightly.

However, Logan is not the only Paul Brother to make headlines and potentially cross the lines, or to bring up issues related to mental health. The younger brother, Jake, has also been viewed and cited as a troll in his own right. But more than that, he has also been associated with the words "sociopath" and "psychopath" for his behaviors and seeming lack of empathy toward his "friends" in videos (Dawson, 2018). With a therapist tagging along for Shane Dawson's six-part documentary on the younger of the brothers, many may watch and start to question the mental health and well-being of this "celebrity" with little understanding of these terms and/or psychology as a whole.

The Paul Brothers are by no means the only YouTube personalities to bring up issues related to trolling or mental health. We could easily discuss Colleen Ballinger (2020) or John Green (2017) vlogging their personal struggles with obsessive compulsive disorder (OCD). Or Joey Graceffa (2014) and his former partner Daniel Preda (2019), on their personal dealings with anxiety and depression symptoms. YouTube has become a place for anyone and everyone to discuss anything and everything, be it makeup or their therapy session. And people tune in to it all. Due to all this, it seemed fitting to make YouTube and the Internet our next project.

To do this, we first considered the "characters" of YouTube and the popular channels/users of the fandom, just as we have with the studies discussed in the previous chapters. We delved into the corners of YouTube to examine everyone from the Paul Brothers to the Vlogbrothers, JoJo Siwa to Miranda Sings, The Try Guys to jacksepticeye, and everything in between. We included the vloggers, the makeup artists, the gamers, the cooks, and the "internetainers" to formulate a list of over 200 diverse YouTube/Internet content creators (for examples of these people, see appendix C).

Each of these creators represent their own, often boisterous, personality in the media. As with many of our studies, we were curious about the differences among the fans. Did more extraverted individuals prefer the likes of the Paul Brothers? Were fans of Buzzfeed Unsolved higher in openness? How about those of fans who have remained devoted to PewDiePie? By this point, we had been using the Big Five and Dark Triad to measures personality traits for many years and chose to continue to do so with this new study. We ultimately wanted to know about the personality traits and as well as the behaviors of Internet fans.

For this, we felt it was important to tackle two fairly debated "behaviors" of the Internet: trolling (obviously, as we have already discussed) and overuse/addiction. The idea of addiction, or problematic engagement with the Internet and its related apps has been growing with the increase in usage and options. With more people logging in rather than sitting down in front of their cable tv, addiction to the Internet has been a controversial topic for multiple reasons. First, there has been the debate about whether to even consider it an "addiction" since addictions have typically been defined by mental health fields as something involving a substance and not a behavior. The most recent version of the Diagnostic and Statistical Manual of Mental Disorders (DSM-5; American Psychiatric Association, 2013) has moved away from this notion with the inclusion of Gambling Disorder under the "Substance-Related and Addictive Disorders" section. This is the first time that a behavioral addiction has been included with those involving substances.

The criteria for Pathological Gambling Disorder have been used as a basis for recommended criteria for Internet addiction. However, Beard and Wolf (2001) proposed a modification in these criteria because it was felt that strictly modeling the criteria after Gambling Disorder allows for just about everything to be an "addiction." For example, a new mother may need increased amounts of time with her baby for excitement, feel restless or irritable when away from the baby, can't control or cut back on her time with the child, and is often pre-occupied with baby. However, we would probably not say that this mother is addicted to her child.

By requiring that all five criteria listed be present, the basis for a problem can be set. However, including one of the remaining three criteria (see table 6.1) indicates that there is something problematic occurring because the person

Table 6.1. Beard and Wolf's proposed criteria (2001)

All the following (1–5) must be present:

1. Is preoccupied with the Internet (thinks about previous online activity or anticipate next online session).
2. Needs to use the Internet with increased amounts of time in order to achieve satisfaction.
3. Has made unsuccessful efforts to control, cut back, or stop Internet use.
4. Is restless, moody, depressed, or irritable when attempting to cut down or stop Internet use.
5. Has stayed online longer than originally intended.

At least one of the following:

1. Has jeopardized or risked the loss of a significant relationship, job, educational or career opportunity because of the Internet.
2. Has lied to family members, therapist, or others to conceal the extent of involvement with the Internet.
3. Uses the Internet as a way of escaping from problems or of relieving a dysphoric mood (e.g., feelings of helplessness, guilt, anxiety, depression).

is jeopardizing or risking loss, lying, or using the Internet as a way to escape from problems. For our research, we used Beard and Wolf's proposed criteria for Internet addiction and utilized their criteria as survey questions to evaluate whether a person would meet the standards to be classified as addicted to the Internet. This left us wondering, how would our sample compare?

All participants were presented with the Big Five Inventory (John and Srivastava, 1999), each of the three components of the Dark Triad (Machiavellianism as measured by the MACH-IV: Yetişer, 2014), psychopathy as measured by the SRP-III (Paulhus, Neumann, and Hare, 2009), narcissism as measured by the NPI (Raskin and Hall, 1981), the Global Assessment of Internet Trolling (GAIT; Buckels, Trapnell, and Paulhus, 2014), the Internet addiction criteria (Beard and Wolf, 2001), demographics (see appendix A for a list of these), and more than 100 YouTube creators who were alphabetized and then randomized (see appendix C for a list and discussion about these). Participants went through the list and rated each YouTuber on a scale of one to seven as to the degree to which they "liked" the characters (1 = Strongly dislike while 7 = Strongly like). We did allow for individuals to skip (and not rate) YouTubers that they did not know, thus preventing skew.

A total of 104 individuals completed the survey through Qualtrics (http://www.qualtrics.com) (Qualtrics, Provo, UT)). Of these, 29 percent identified as male, 69 percent identified as female, and 2 percent identified as one of the "other" options that we provided. Most identified as heterosexual (82 percent), but we did have good LGBTQIA+ identification with this smaller sample size (5 percent identified as gay or lesbian, 8 percent identified as bisexual, and 5 percent identified in one of our "other" categories). About 91 percent of our sample consider themselves fans of Internet media (games, videos, memes, comment threads, etc.), and 75 percent identified as fans of YouTube.

To our surprise, 9 percent of our participant pool met our criteria (operational definition) for Internet addiction. To give that some context, according to the National Survey on Drug Use and Health (NSDUH; SAMHSA, 2018) 5.8 percent of those 18 and older had an alcohol use disorder, and between 8 to 12 percent of the population develops an opioid use disorder (Vowles, McEntee, Julnes, et al. 2015). It is estimated that around 13.7 percent of US adults are cigarette smokers (Creamer, Wang, Babb, et al., 2019). It is evident that the maladaptive use of the Internet is just as significant as many substance disorders.

Our most liked YouTubers, in order, were fairly predictable based on number of subscribers and platform accessibility (based on when the dataset was collected): Jenna Marbles, Shane Dawson, Bad Lip Reading, Rhett and Link, Trisha Paytas, Keith (Try Guys), Julien Solomita, Ned (Try Guys), Eugene

(Try Guys), Zach (Try Guys), and Shane and Ryan (Buzzfeed Unsolved). Our least liked YouTubers contained some surprises: Logan Paul, Jake Paul, JoJo Siwa (we went from the Paul Brothers to the teen queen of the elementary school set), Tré Melvin, De'aara and Ken 4 Life, Bryan Le (RiceGum), Andrea's Choice, Arin and Dan (GameGrumps), and KSI.

We performed a series of standard multiple regressions using the eight sub-components of personality as our predictor variables for both our most liked and least liked lists. As always, a Bonferroni correction was conducted to counter the number of analyses conducted and to protect our Type I error rate; the significance level has been lowered to from $p < .05$ to $p < .005$ to determine significance.

On our most liked list only Ned, Zach, and Keith from the Try Guys demonstrated a relationship between liking and personality with openness as a marginally significant predictor ($p = .05$). The least liked list was a little more interesting, although these were all also only marginally significant. Liking Logan Paul, who many, as we have discussed, consider a real-life troll with his endeavors, was predicted by higher scores on both Machiavellianism and psychopathy. As a reminder, these are two of the three components of the Dark Triad. Liking Tre Melvin was predicted by higher Machiavellianism scores and lower neuroticism scores. Andrea's Choice was predicted by lower scores on narcissism, openness, and conscientiousness, and the Merrell Twins were predicted by lower scores on narcissism and neuroticism.

YouTube and the culture surrounding it is similar to the other areas of popular culture we have studied and discussed in previous chapters, and you can see specific traits factoring into character preference. However, YouTube is different in a very interesting, critical way. We know that many Internet and social media sites use algorithms to keep people on the site, app, and/or Internet. How often have you planned to go on the Internet for a particular reason or with the intention of being on for a few minutes, only to "go down the rabbit hole" and before you know it, you have been online for much longer than you expected? Young (1998) actually referred to this phenomenon as the "terminal time warp." A person who is already susceptible to engaging in problematic Internet use may be at even more risk when engaging with these types of web sites or streaming content. Of course, another implication of engaging with the Internet in a maladaptive manner has already been discussed with the potential of these behaviors to impact a person's daily life and their ability to function in various environments, roles, and relationships from school, to employment, to taking care of children, to problems with friends and partners.

In the future, we need to examine updates to the criteria for Gambling Disorder and see what may need adjusted to the criteria for Internet addiction. This will allow for our results to continue to mirror designated criteria for other behavioral addictions. Examining what factors, if any, about the Internet may make people who are susceptible to addiction more likely to be at risk for developing problematic Internet use is something that needs to be further investigated. We also need to explore factors related to the Internet that may allow for trolling and bullying, such as the sense of anonymity when online and the ease of avoiding confrontation after making a scandalous remark by simply logging off. The Internet isn't going away. While there are numerous positives that the Internet has brought to us, the mental health field needs to study ways to encourage and promote healthy online behavior and interactions in an effort to be proactive to prevent the development of a problem rather than being reactive and dealing with the addiction after the fact.

As we have said, the Internet is here to stay, and it will continue to influence and grow. It will unquestionably change. It will most certainly evolve. We know things in popular culture move quickly, and as we were collecting participants for this dataset, we saw some big shifts in popularity. (We would wager that while you are reading this many of the individuals that we are discussing or referencing will have fallen out of favor.) At the time of this study, TikTok had not gained momentum in the way that it has since the COVID-19 pandemic. Will TikTok overthrow the mogul of YouTube just as YouTube may have dethroned MTV, just as MTV seems to have "killed" radio programming? Things change.

Sometimes that change can lead to the "cancellation" of something. "Cancel culture," as this is often referred to, has grown . . . especially in 2020. Just as TikTok grew in popularity, its use and access was threatened to be banned in the United States, or in essence cancelled, by Donald Trump. This of course followed on the heels of actress Sarah Cooper posting multiple videos making fun of him, which followed shortly after many users trolled his rallies through the app (Emmrich, 2020). Interestingly, this TikTok news comes after many of the previously mentioned YouTube creators were "cancelled" in their own right. In 2020, we saw Jenna Marbles (the most liked creator at the time of our study) choose to take an extended break from her own channel, in some ways "cancelling" herself, due to old content possibly containing negative stereotypes. Similarly, Shane Dawson (the second most liked) faced backlash for potentially discriminatory content on his own channel and was completely demonetized at the time by YouTube (Alexander, 2020). Regardless of the example, cancel culture has consequences and continues to grow in its impact on popular culture.

Moving forward, we would like not only a larger sample size for a study of this nature but to also explore the addition and impact of cancel culture. This will mean that we will need to be extra cognizant when exploring cancel culture given the negative content associated with it, including spam comments and the influence that it has on how much we like a given individual (be it YouTuber, character, or show). This is even commercialized as a frequent segment on the late-night show, *Jimmy Kimmel Live!*, which popularizes this concept by having celebrities read mean tweets about themselves (Kimmel, Kellison, Gray, Leiderman, Schrift, and DeLuca, 2020). While this is done for laughs, you can identify how hurtful and damaging these remarks could be when made through online platforms that allow for some sense of anonymity. These are statements that would rarely, if ever, be uttered to a person when face-to-face. This is even more important in terms of responses and attitudes toward those who identify as part of a minority group based on racial-ethnic diversity, sexual orientation and identity, disability, and age. Of course, gender is also a factor that may incite this cancel culture and with the rise of the #MeToo movement, we are being made more aware of the differences and of how females are treated versus their male counterparts (Spence, Helmreich, and Stapp, 1978).

REFERENCES

Alexander, J. (2020, July 2). White YouTube creators struggle to address past use of racist characters. The Verge. Retrieved from: https://www.theverge.com/2020/7/2/21306858/shane-dawson-jenna-marbles-youtube-blackface-racism-content. American Psychiatric Association. (2013). Diagnostic and statistical manual of mental disorders: DSM–5. Washington, D.C: American Psychiatric Association.

Ballinger, C. [Colleen Vlogs]. (2020, March 26). *My OCD was bad last night* [Video File]. Retrieved from: https://www.youtube.com/watch?v=CANTdkuBrTk.

Beard, K. W., and Wolf, E. M. (2001). Modification in the proposed diagnostic criteria for Internet addiction. *CyberPsychology & Behavior, 4*(3), 377–382.

Buckels, E. E., Trapnell, P. D., and Paulhus. D. L. (2014). Trolls just want to have fun. *Personality and Individual Differences 67*, 97–102.

Dawson, S. [shane]. (2018, October 18). *Inside the mind of Jake Paul* [Video Files]. Retrieved from: https://www.youtube.com/watch?v=de9iiaxLEgM&list=RDde9iiaxLEgM&start_radio=1&t=0.

Craker, N., and March, E. (2016). The dark side of Facebook: The dark tetrad, negative social potency, and trolling behaviours. *Personality and Individual Differences, 102*, 79–84.

Creamer M. R., Wang T. W., Babb S., Cullen, K. A., Day, H., Willis, G., Jamal, A., and Neff, L. (2019). Tobacco product use and cessation indicators among adults—United States, 2018. *Morbidity and Mortality Weekly Report, 68*(45), 1013–1019.

Emmrich, S. (2020, Aug. 1). Is Sarah Cooper the reason Donald Trump wants to ban TikTok? Vogue. Retrieved from: https://www.vogue.com/article/is-sarah-cooper-the-reason-donald-trump-wants-to-ban-tik-tok.

Graceffa, J. [Joey Graceffa]. (2014, July 23). *Real Talk* [Video File]. Retrieved from: https://www.youtube.com/watch?v=rPfSfpPmDGY.

Green, J. [Vlogbrothers]. (2017, July 25). *What OCD is like (for me)* [Video File]. Retrieved from https://www.youtube.com/watch?v=jNEUz9v5RYo.

Hardaker, C. (2010). Trolling in asynchronous computermediated communication: From user discussions to academic definitions. *Journal of Politeness Research, 6*(2) pp. 215-242.

John, O.P., and Srivastava, S. (1999). The Big-Five trait taxonomy: History, measurement, and theoretical perspectives. In L. A. Pervin and O. P. John (Eds.), *Handbook of personality: Theory and research* (Vol. 2, pp. 102–138). New York: Guilford Press.

Kimmel, J., Kellison, D., Gray, D., Leiderman, J., Schrift, J., and DeLuca, D. ([Producers]) (2020). *Jimmy Kimmel Live!* Hollywood, CA: ABC.

Logan Paul: Outrage over YouTuber's Japan dead man video. (2018, Jan. 2). BBC News. Retrieved from: https://www.bbc.com/news/world-asia-42538495.

Paulhus, D. L., Neumann, C. S., and Hare, R. D. (2009). *Manual for the Self-Report Psychopathy scale*. Toronto: Multi-Health Systems.

Preda, D. [Mister Preda]. (2019, January 13). *Opening up about a few things* [Video File]. Retrieved from: https://www.youtube.com/watch?v=Jjfo5akveXA.

Qualtrics software, Version XM of Qualtrics. Copyright © 2018 Qualtrics. Qualtrics and all other Qualtrics product or service names are registered trademarks or trademarks of Qualtrics, Provo, UT, USA. (http://www.qualtrics.com).

Raskin, R. N., and Hall, C. S. (1981). The Narcissistic Personality Inventory: Alternative form reliability and further evidence of construct validity. *Journal of Personality Assessment, 45*, 159–160.

SAMHSA. (2018). National Survey on Drug Use and Health (NSDUH). Table 5.4A—Alcohol Use Disorder in Past Year among Persons Aged 12 or Older, by Age Group and Demographic Characteristics: Numbers in Thousands, 2017 and 2018. Retrieved from: https://www.samhsa.gov/data/sites/default/files/cbhsq-reports/NSDUHDetailedTabs2018R2/NSDUHDetTabsSect5pe2018.htm#tab5-4a.

Spence, J. T., Helmreich, R., and Stapp, J. (1978). A short version of the Attitudes toward Women Scale (AWS). *Bulletin of the Psychonomic Society, 2*, 219–220.

Vowles, K. E., McEntee M. L., Julnes P. S., Frohe, T., Ney, J. P., and van der Goes, D. N. (2015). Rates of opioid misuse, abuse, and addiction in chronic pain: a systematic review and data synthesis. *Pain, 156*(4), 569–576. doi:10.1097/01.j.pain.0000460357.01998.fl.

Weiss, G. (2018, Nov. 19). Logan Paul headlines 'flat earth' convention in what appears to be a troll. Tubefilter. Retrieved from: https://www.tubefilter.com/2018/11/19/logan-paul-flat-earth-troll/.

Yetişer, B. (2014). Do all roads lead to Rome? The moderating role of culture and age in predicting construal level on Machiavellianism. *Journal of Yasar University, 9*(36), 6328–6337.

Young, K. S. (1998). *Caught in the Net: How to recognize the signs of Internet addiction and a winning strategy for recovery*. Hoboken, NJ: Wiley.

Chapter Seven

The Role of Women
and the #MeToo Movement

A woman was finally on top! Well, sort of . . . 2019 marked the first time we had a female identifying character/personality top the most liked spot on one of our lists with Jenna Marbles being our most liked YouTuber. This is something that took over seven years' worth of data collection to achieve. Seven years of watching beloved idols such as (Princess to General) Leia Organa (*Star Wars*), Hermione Granger (*Harry Potter*), and more fall short. *Seven years.*

This should not have been all that surprising . . . considering Black Widow (*Marvel Universe*) will have waited over a decade by the time her solo film is released and Wonder Woman (*DC Universe*) had to play with the boys (Batman and Superman [*DC Universe*]) before she was allowed to lead her own film (Roven, Snyder, and Snyder, 2016). Likewise, it took over 25 years for a woman to captain a Star Fleet ship, with Captain Kathryn Janeway taking the helm (*Star Trek: Voyager;* Berman, 1995). Similarly, to what we haves seen in our political system, a person of color was leading a *Star Trek* show (*Star Trek: Deep Space Nine*; Berman, 1993) just as a black male was elected president before a woman has ever been elected. Women have traditionally not been given the lead in popular culture. While many have been showcased in the main cast of many popular franchises (*Star Wars, Star Trek, Avengers,* etc.), they usually are cast aside in some manner while the male lead takes center stage. And when they are cast as the head of the franchise, like we see in the newest *Star Wars* movies with Rey, they give the males the attention when it comes to merchandising and publicity (Whitten, 2017). There has long been an unspoken rule that the world of superheroes, fantasy, and science fiction is a boys' club.

Not only is it a boy's club, but female identifying characters often serve as little more than a sexy love interest or small blip in the plot for many popular films and comics. Or, if they are featured as something more, they still are utilized as sex objects in one way or another. This can be seen in one of the original poster designs for the first Avengers film where all of the main cast is together, looking strong and showcasing their power. Well, all but Natasha. Black Widow, unlike all the male identifying characters, was contorted by the artist so she was twisted in such a way as to show off her backside. The rest of the Avengers Team is shown flexing their muscles and engaged in action of some form (MacDonald, 2011). This speaks to the issue that these female characters are often sexualized, unrealistic, and/or unimportant to the main plot in many ways.

This double standard in how women are represented can also be seen in print. The Hawkeye Initiative (n.d.) is a satirical Tumblr account that poses Hawkeye (*Marvel Universe*) in various positions that his female counterparts have been drawn to compare how the original artwork has women in ridiculous and sometimes impossible poses. The sexualization of the female body is obvious when a male, who is often not sexualized in this manner, is replacing the woman. As comic book writer Kelly Sue DeConnick has said in interviews, "if you can remove a female character from your plot and replace her with a sexy lamp and your story still works, you're a hack" (Joshua, 2013, para 12). Unfortunately, there have been many "hacks" out there when it comes to female representation.

Representation is important, as we have already discussed in previous chapters (chapters 4 and 5). Regardless of the medium, be it the nightly news or the latest superhero blockbuster, it is once again clear that representation matters. Media often depicts real world and relevant insights, just as we have discussed with our politics study. Characters are shown behaving as many in the real world would, be it the mundane such as eating or drinking, or something more aspirational like going out with someone or obtaining the dream job. Nan's (2011) research regarding cultivation theory has suggested that prolonged exposure to popular culture images can alter the viewer's opinions and perceptions, so that they align with that of the characters or messages in the books, movies, or television programs in which the individual engages. Even when it is under the guise of a Superman-type working his day job with his girl to cover up for his superhero antics . . . it shows opinions and perceptions on daily life. At the end of the day, television and movies have the potential to shape opinions and perceptions of consumers and to influence their social reality.

This is particularly important when considering how female identifying individuals are depicted. With many appearing as either the damsel in distress or the sexualized hero, what are viewers taking away? Previous research suggests that female identifying characters are given little complexity in terms of their storylines and often portrayed in unrealistic images. This in turn has the potential to alter how audience members view gender norms and the roles of females (Pennell and Behm-Morawitz, 2015).

We voice all of this to say, women are not always viewed in the same way as their male counterparts. Be it in regard to grander scales such as a presidential election, or with everyday issues such as the gender pay gap, differences continue to be made between men and women. This perhaps can be seen all too well with the rise of #MeToo. Alyssa Milano started a movement in 2017 against sexual harassment by tweeting out against then famous movie producer Harvey Weinstein. Milano's tweet created a spark of retweets and replies of over 12 million within 24 hours . . . all with the #MeToo in solidarity (Hosterman, Johnson, Stouffer, and Herring, 2018). It was becoming increasingly obvious that those who identify as female were being treated differently and being hurt in the process.

Since then, we have seen this play out in various mediums and facets. News has blasted Harvey Weinstein, showing clips of him slinking out from the courthouse. Movies based on stories of real-life harassment such as *Bombshell* have hit theaters (Randolph and Roach, 2019). Television has even tackled the topic through a talking cartoon horse in the Netflix series *BoJack Horseman*, having the lead character, an anamorphic horse acting in a starring role of a crime drama, choke his co-star/girlfriend and possibly seduce underage women (Bob-Waksberg, 2020). Since the 2017 movement began, people have been turning their attention to the issue and to attitudes toward women becoming a buzz topic in their own way. However, this does not always lead to change as we continue to hear stories from both inside and out of Hollywood. With women being snubbed for the Best Director Oscar in 2020 and documentaries depicting Jeffrey Epstein's alleged abuse, it is still an important issue. For all these reasons, we too turned our attention to the often-disregarded world of female identifying characters. We would like to pause for a moment to highlight that we have been and will continue to use "female identifying" as well as "male identifying" throughout this chapter to be more inclusive regardless of biological sex.

All participants were presented with the Attitudes toward Women Scale: Short Version (AWS) (Spence, Helmreich, and Stapp, 1978). The AWS: Short Version has been proven to be a reliable measure, with "Cronbach's alpha in the mid .80's or higher" and a high correlation to the longer version of the survey (Spence and Hahn, 1997). Previously discussed measures were included as well: the Big Five Inventory (John and Srivastava, 1999); each of the three components of the Dark Triad with Machiavellianism as measured by the MACH-IV (Yetişer, 2014), psychopathy as measured by the SRP-III (Paulhus, Neumann, and Hare, 2009), and narcissism as measured by the NPI (Raskin and Hall, 1981) the Global Assessment of Internet Trolling (GAIT)

(Buckels, Trapnell, and Paulhus, 2014), demographics (see appendix A for a discussion of these), and 200-plus female identifying characters and individuals and approximately 50 male identifying individuals (see appendix C for discussion on these).

As usual, participants went through the list on Qualtrics (http://www.qualtrics.com) (Qualtrics, Provo, UT)) and rated each character on a scale of one to seven as to the degree to which they "liked" the characters (1 = Strongly dislike while 7 = Strongly like). We focused on female identifying characters from across a span of genres and popularity periods (Marvel, DC Comics, Disney, Television, etc.). We did allow for individuals to skip (and not rate) characters that they did not know. This prevented characters and teams (see appendix D and chapter 9 for a discussion on fandoms) from being skewed by lesser known members.

A total of 143 individuals completed the survey. Of these, 19.6 percent identified as male, 78.3 percent identified as female, and .7 percent identified as one of the "other" options that we provided. Most identified as heterosexual (82.5 percent), but we did have good LGBTQIA+ identification with this smaller sample size (4.2 percent identified as gay or lesbian and 7 percent identified as bisexual). About 85.3 percent of our sample consider themselves fans of Internet media (games, videos, memes, comment threads, etc.) and 58 percent identified that they post comments on the Internet. Surprisingly, 8.4 percent self-identified as considering themselves to be Internet trolls.

All analyses were completed examining all eight sub-components of personality along with the AWS and the GAIT scales. As always, a Bonferroni correction was conducted to counter the number of analyses conducted and to protect our Type I error rate; the significance level has been lowered to from $p < .05$ to $p < .005$ to determine significance.

The first thing that we did was to explore the relationships between each of our measures (minus the GAIT) with the Attitudes toward Women Scale (AWS) as our focus. As a reminder, "A high score indicates a profeminist, egalitarian attitude while a low score indicates a traditional, conservative attitude" (Spence, Helmreich and Stapp, 1978). There was not a significant relationship between scores on the AWS and scores on neuroticism ($r = .083$), extraversion ($r = .045$), or Machiavellianism ($r = .098$). There was a significant, positive correlation between openness ($r = .332$), agreeableness ($r = .637$), and conscientiousness ($r = .362$). Higher scores on these three measures usually indicated a higher score on the AWS and a more equal, or democratic, view on women. The AWS was negatively correlated with narcissism ($r = -.465$), psychopathy ($r = -.563$), and the GAIT ($r = -.362$). Higher scores on these three measures usually indicated a lower score on the AWS. These negative correlations seem to support the idea from chapter

4 that several of the components of the Dark Triad are more associated with traditional, conservative views. These views seem to extend to attitudes about women.

We then performed a series of stepwise regressions to explore the relationships between personality traits, the GAIT, and the AWS in an effort to determine if these components work to predict how much participants might like certain characters. Perhaps unsurprisingly then, it is the attitudes toward women that dominate those predictions. In fact, all but one of the female identifying characters that were ran (and produced a significant model) were predicted by higher attitudes toward women. Five of the characters that are significantly predicted were *only* predicted by AWS (Wonder Woman, Batwoman [*DC Universe*]), Mystique[1] (*Marvel Universe*), Hermione Granger (*Harry Potter*), and Eleven (*Stranger Things*). Carol Danvers, Jean Grey, Gamora, Storm, and Jessica Jones (all *Marvel Universe*) were all also predicted by higher scores on the AWS but they were also predicted by higher scores on Machiavellianism. Moana (*Disney*) was also more liked by those scoring higher on the AWS along with higher scores on extraversion and neuroticism. The only character that was not predicted by AWS was Cersei Lannister (*Game of Thrones*) (lower levels of agreeableness predict higher levels of liking). It would be interesting to further explore these results for Cersei. She is a character that not only breaks the standard norms for females (she is a queen), but she also breaks several other societal norms (i.e., incest and power prostituting of her children).

All these characters find themselves in leadership roles and represent genres usually dominated by male characters. For every female such as Wonder Woman on a team, we get about four male leads (Batman, Superman, Flash, and Green Lantern—please note that these authors also realize that we could add Aquaman or Martian Manhunter or Cyborg to the Justice League [*DC Universe*] line-up, but the point remains that we could add a number of male identifying characters before adding another female to the line-up).

This begs the question, how do the results for these female identifying characters compare to the more traditional male identifying characters? With regard to our characters, we did not include male identifying examples in our survey. However, we did posit the question of how men and women who have been public about personal struggles with mental health related topics would compare to one another. Part of the list we created for this study (see appendix C for examples) included women and men who have been known to struggle in their personal lives with mental health related conditions, be it anything from substance use disorder to depression.

We did this in order to better understand how fans view these individuals, much as we wanted to understand how they viewed our female identifying characters. At the time we were creating this list, the authors were noticing a striking difference in how the media was discussing two separate drug overdoses that had occurred within weeks of one another. Demi Lovato was largely being shamed and guilted for "choosing" to be addicted to substances whereas Mac Miller's overdose death seemed to cause a casting of blame and anger toward his ex-girlfriend, Ariana Grande. The women involved were being blamed. The men were given sympathy (Virzi, 2018). The media was creating a striking difference in how they covered a very sad, difficult topic.

This of course is not the first time this has happened. Or the first time difficult personal matters that celebrities experience have been blasted across the magazines. Decades before, we saw Charlie Sheen's spiral televised every week. Before that, we saw that Robert Downey, Jr. was more famous for wearing an orange jumpsuit than his now infamous Iron Man suit. Media coverage of these issues often takes on a similar problem as we see in how women themselves are depicted, often unrealistically.

All of this is a future direction and brought up questions of representation and how female and male identifying individuals are viewed. However, it was not the only question that we took away from this chapter. Both Britani and April were quite sad that several of our "favorite" characters were not significant, and we could not talk about them. Characters like Bella Swan (*Twilight*), Peggy Carter (*Marvel Universe*), Buffy Summers (*Buffy the Vampire Slayer*), and Ursula (*Disney*) were not significant. And please do not get Keith started on his feelings about Minnie Mouse (*Disney*). This did lead us to a big conclusion . . . we were feeling nostalgic, and that nostalgia only intensified as we moved into the "Great Pause" of the 2020 COVID-19 pandemic.

NOTE

1. These characters were only marginally significant. They met the $p < .05$ benchmark but not the $p < .005$ benchmark.

REFERENCES

Berman, R. (Executive Producer). (1993). *Star Trek: Deep Space Nine*. [Motion Picture]. Los Angeles, CA: Syndication.

Berman, R. (Executive Producer). (1995). *Star Trek: Voyager*. [Motion Picture]. Los Angeles, CA: Syndication.

Bob-Waksberg, R. (Executive Producer). (2020). *BoJack Horseman* [Television Series]. United States: Netflix.

Buckels, E., Trapnell, P., and Paulhus, D. (2014). Trolls just want to have fun. *Personality and Individual Differences, 67*, 97–102.

Hosterman, A., Johnson, N., Stouffer, R., and Herring, S. (2018). Twitter, social support messages and the #MeToo movement. *The Journal of Social Media in Society, 7*(2), 69–91.

John, O. P., and Srivastava, S. (1999). The Big-Five trait taxonomy: History, measurement, and theoretical perspectives. In L. A. Pervin and O. P. John (Eds.), *Handbook of personality: Theory and research* (Vol. 2, pp. 102–138). New York: Guilford Press.

Joshua (2013). Kelly Sue DeConnick talks Captain Marvel, Pretty Deadly, and the sexy lamp test. IGN. Retrieved from: https://www.ign.com/articles/2013/06/20/kelly-sue-deconnick-talks-captain-marvel-pretty-deadly-and-the-sexy-lamp-test.

MacDonald, H. (2011, November 28). *Gender swap Avengers poster gives us lots of butt.* The Beat. Retrieved from: https://www.comicsbeat.com/gender-swap-avengers-poster-gives-us-lots-of-butt/.

Nan, X. (2011). Influence of television on viewing and sensation seeking on adolescents' unrealistic perceptions about smoking and smokers: Evidence from a national survey. *Mass Communication and Society, 14*, 643–665.

Paulhus, D. L., Neumann, C. S., and Hare, R. D. (2009). *Manual for the Self-Report Psychopathy scale.* Toronto: Multi-Health Systems.

Pennell, H. and Behm-Morawitz, E. (2015). The empowering (super) heroine? The effects of sexualized female characters in superhero films on women. *Sex Roles, 72*, 211–220.

Qualtrics software, Version XM of Qualtrics. Copyright © 2018 Qualtrics. Qualtrics and all other Qualtrics product or service names are registered trademarks or trademarks of Qualtrics, Provo, UT, USA. (http://www.qualtrics.com).

Randolph, C. (Writer), and Roach, J. (Director). (2019). *Bombshell* [Motion Picture]. United States: Lionsgate.

Raskin, R. N., and Hall, C. S. (1981). The Narcissistic Personality Inventory: Alternative form reliability and further evidence of construct validity. *Journal of Personality Assessment, 45*, 159–160.

Roven, C., Snyder, D. (Producers), and Snyder, Z. (Director). (2016). *Batman v. Superman: Dawn of Justice* [Motion Picture]. United States: Warner Bros. Pictures.

Spence, J. and Hahn, E. (1997). The attitudes toward women scale and attitude change in college students. *Psychology of Women Quarterly, 21*, 17–34.

Spence, J. T., Helmreich, R., and Stapp, J. (1978). A short version of the Attitudes toward Women Scale (AWS). *Bulletin of the Psychonomic Society, 2*, 219–220.

The Hawkeye Initiative (n.d.) Retrieved from https://thehawkeyeinitiative.tumblr.com/.

Virzi, J. (2018, September 12). Responses to Demi Lovato and Mac Miller's overdoses highlight an alarming truth. The Mighty. Retrieved from: https://themighty.com/2018/09/mac-miller-demi-lovato-ariana-grande-addiction-sexist-responses/.

Whitten, S. (2017). This 'Star Wars' character altered the toy industry forever. CNBC. Retrieved from: https://www.cnbc.com/2017/02/27/this-star-wars-character-altered-the-toy-industry-forever.html.

Yetişer, B. (2014). Do all roads lead to Rome? The moderating role of culture and age in predicting construal level on Machiavellianism. *Journal of Yasar University, 9*(36), 6328–6337.

Chapter Eight

All the Nostalgia

Generational Shifts in Personality and in Cartoon Character Preferences

As you may be noticing, each of us writing this really do have our favorites. These favorites have been driving our research in many ways since the beginning. We have fought for our picks to be included in the research lists and debated the merits of each item many times over the last decade. They are our characters. The characters that hold a special place in our hearts and bring up special memories or a sense of nostalgia for us. Keith's love of all things Mickey Mouse brings back memories of a trip to Disney with his siblings. Britani's obsession with Marvel brings up thoughts of going to the original Spider-Man movies with her father. April sighing at each new addition she would have to analyze while making sure every *Lord of the Rings* character made its way onto the list because those were her favorite books from childhood. We all have our "things." Numerous factors, franchises, and fandoms that influences how we approach each of our studies and how we craft our character lists each year. Things that hold special memories for each of us.

As we came out of what we affectionally refer to as the "Great Event of 2016" (see the next chapter for a broader discussion of this) and saw how adding Disney characters into the mix greatly impacted our findings, we found ourselves going back to those nostalgic, most-loved characters. Not only were we doing that, we were also seeing a general rise in nostalgia across popular culture, as a whole. Reboots and sequels were starting to grow and take center stage, be it in regard to large franchises like *Star Wars* or small screen classics like *DuckTales*. Favorites from previous decades were making a resurgence and continue to find footing with fans, new and old.

Nostalgia is often regarded as a sense of longing for the past or feelings revolving around the past, and it appears to be "king" in regard to comebacks. It evokes positive emotions through memory and can take almost any type of form (e.g., items, toys, collectables, clothes, etc.) related to childhood or special times in one's life. Nostalgia provides meaning and connection from the past to the present (Sedikides and Wildschut, 2018). It creates a warm feeling in individuals and connects people to those they love or times in their lives that hold importance. For this reason, nostalgia and popular culture seem to go hand in hand.

With popular culture comes a sense of spectacle and nostalgia, and offers something for everyone (Danesi, 2012). Media, especially pop culture, provide a sense of escape for people, an outlet for one to forget his or her or their life for a few hours at a time. Yet pop culture is more than that. It is an outlet that allows viewers to establish a form of emotional investment in something, much as they would a personal relationship (Greenwood, 2009). It is something of its own.

Various disciplines and academics have tried to theorize why people engage with popular culture. In a sense, media associated with popular culture often depicts an aspect of the real world and offers insight into daily life as a result. Television characters are shown as behaving as an individual in his or her or their normal life would, doing everything from the mundane, such as eating or drinking, to something more aspirational, like earning a dream job. Although they can obviously be dramatized and are fictional in nature, they can be a form of socialization for individuals and often act as a socialization agent (Russell and Russell, 2009). In many ways, television and movies persuade viewers that the messages and the worlds they depict are an accurate reflection of the modern world around the viewer (Shrum. 1999). This, in turn, shapes the perceptions of those consumers of popular culture and the associated media, essentially shaping the social reality for them.

As we discussed in previous chapters, Nan's (2011) research regarding cultivation theory has suggested that prolonged exposure to popular culture images can alter the viewer's opinions and perceptions. As a result, they can then align with that of the characters or messages in the books, movies, or television programs with which the individual engages. This has been illustrated through studies questioning the perceived prevalence of violence. Participants who reported watching more hours of television were also more likely to overestimate the prevalence of violence at night compared to those who watched little television (Nan, 2011).

People accept the media and the messages depicted in these fictionalized worlds. They can connect to the characters and take on their perspectives in doing so (Moyer-Guse and Nabi, 2010). Essentially, the audience forms relationships to the characters, no matter the media—from screen to books. Horton and Wohl initially described this relationship as a parasocial relationship where an individual forms a pseudo-friendship with a fictional character or media personality (1956). Popular culture mimics aspects of human nature and everyday life, even when the genres present unreal versions of that life via superheroes and imaginary worlds. The characters provide examples of how problems, relationships, and family dynamics play out at the fictional level, for good or bad. The viewer gains information, whether consciously or not, on the problem, and that information can be later applied to his or her or their real life (Fisher and Salmon, 2012).

Representation matters, as can be seen with successful films such as *Black Panther* and *Crazy Rich Asians*. Even with these successes, there is still a lack of representation for many other marginalized or minority groups, and these depictions often result in backlash. The inclusion of the significant diversity within our world has been (and continues to be) the basis for boycotts, arguments, and even the misconception that there are things such as the "gay agenda" being pushed upon or normalized for the children in our society. This can be illustrated by campaigns like "One Million Moms," with 4,796 Twitter followers (1milmoms, n.d.) as of the writing of this book, boycotting Disney because of a single gay character in both *Beauty and the Beast* or *Onward* (Keller, 2020). Interestingly, neither of these characters are "main" characters, and these scenes involving inclusivity are relatively brief.

As an individual partakes in some form of popular culture, be it watching television or movies or reading books, that person uses the prior knowledge he or she or they may already have about the character to make judgments (Giles, 2002). For those who have formed a parasocial relationship with a character, it extends beyond the end credits or the final page of the book. The individual continues to analyze the judgments made during that initial experience; some may experience rejection by doing so if their peer or social group does not agree or dislikes the character (Horton and Wohl, 1956). For example, despite its popularity in the past, mention of the book and movie series *Twilight* (Meyers, 2011) in conversations has anecdotally brought about strong negative reactions with moans and rolling of the eyes from audience members. In 2020, we see a change once again with the love, or hate, relationship with *Twilight* as Meyers has since published a continuation of the story in *Midnight Sun* to many positive reviews. The waves of popularity, even in one fandom, can be jarring as they ebb and flow over time. For someone who still shows a strong preference toward the characters in the story, such reactions could provide a sense of dissonance among friends.

However, many still take these relationships with the characters further by discussing them with others. Just as we reviewed in chapter 7, due to technological advances and the prevalence of both social media and fan websites, conversations are no longer restricted to personal (or in-person) social groups. As Branch, Wilson, and Agnew discuss in their 2013 work, Facebook and Twitter allow not only interaction with other audience members but also with media figures involved in creating and bringing characters to life. These interactions lend to a deeper experience and continued conversation (Branch, Wilson, and Agnew, 2013). Social media allows a fan to read not only posts set up to mimic the fictional characters but also the actors messaging about their characters being portrayed in their current or upcoming projects. For example, someone can set up a Twitter account and tweet messages as if he or she is Deadpool (*Marvel Universe*), while at the same time, Ryan Reynolds, the actor behind the character, can also tweet messages about his role in upcoming films. With both, fans can engage with the fandom and feel a sense of connection to not only the actor portraying the character but also the character themself.

Through this, initial opinions can change and continue to develop over time, leading to meaningful thought and interactions (Giles, 2002). It almost mimics aspects of a friendship in that the individual observes the character and then makes interpretations about what they see and hear. The audience member may see the character as a model or someone with whom they seek comfort and counseling, even though the relationship is one-sided as the character does not typically interact with the individual (Horton and Wohl, 1956).

Despite the one-sided nature of the relationship, people become invested and committed to popular characters. Be it traditional heroes or villains, people devote not only their time and attention, but also their money, to following the stories, mediums, and merchandise associated with their favorite character, such as clothing, toys, and memorabilia. The fictional nature notwithstanding, people gain benefit from the parasocial interactions they experience with these characters. Derrick, Gabriel, and Hugenberg (2009) have indicated that engaging in/with popular media, such as watching a favorite television program, can ease negative feelings such as loneliness and is often seen as an outlet by which lonely individuals believe they can improve emotional states and create a sense of belongingness that they feel is lacking. It was found that people felt an improvement in terms of self-esteem and mood even when just thinking about favored television characters. It almost appears as if these relationships with fictional characters mimics a real-life relationship in that sense.

Research on relationships have generally examined questions regarding why people become invested in these characters. Although the majority of the studies have focused on tangible relationships with others, a parasocial relationship can be investigated in similar ways. As Branch, Wilson, and Agnew illustrated in their 2013 study, a parasocial relationship can be compared to an interpersonal relationship in terms of level of investment and satisfaction. By using the investment model, these researchers examined how investment and satisfaction predicted the commitment to a fictional character. In previous research, Arriaga and Agnew (2001) used the model, which hypothesizes that individuals commit to a relationship based upon the satisfaction felt in the relationship, the alternatives available for that relationship, and the level of investment felt. All of these constructs are dependent upon the individual's perception of the relationship and the other partner (Arriaga and Agnew, 2001), thus, lending support for the idea that these relationships to fictional characters have tangible, measurable, and meaningful applications to that person.

Regarding these fictional relationships, the results of the Branch et al. (2013) study have indicated that, much like in real-world interpersonal relationships, the level of investment and the satisfaction felt in the relationship can positively predict the level of commitment to the character. This relationship can be driven by watching characters on television or in movies or following nonfictional characters on social media. In either case, the constructs driving the level of commitment are similar to those that drive interpersonal relationships with individuals in the real world (Branch et al., 2013).

Considering that many may turn to fictional characters and worlds to alleviate negative emotions or to substitute for a perceived lack of relationships in their real lives, it is understandable that people form connections and levels of commitments to popular culture characters. Giles (2002) argued that for some it may be viewed as a normal form of social activity and helps to compensate for loneliness. The character is somewhat integrated into a social network despite the fact that one does not necessarily interact with them in the same manner in which he or she or they communicates with others in that network.

It then appears as if popular culture brings about a sense of relatedness or wish fulfillment through the characters. This brings up the pleasant memories and the warm and fuzzy feelings we had at the time of our first engagement or interaction with these characters back into our lives once again (Hesley and Hesley, 1998). Engagement can be particularly important during dark times in our lives. Or, more recently during the COVID-19 pandemic, as we see Disney+ and other cartoon streaming services continue to add and develop very nostalgic content. As we write this, two of these authors are doing just that and binging the same series (although a series that was popular in different iterations for us in our childhoods but . . . *Scooby-Doo* is always *Scooby-Doo*, no matter the iteration).

However, it is not just movies and television that capitalize on these warm, fuzzy feelings. Many brands and stores have also jumped on the bandwagon. Stores aimed at those in their teens and twenties frequently sell merchandise covered in favorite cartoon characters from various decades of media. Music from the 1970s and the 1980s continue to be requested on the radio. And even books come back around. We frequently look to the past for "comfort food" in the forms of our favorites, whatever those may be.

Nostalgia is comfort. Previous research highlights the impact nostalgia can have on well-being during stressful times. It can act as a buffer and even protect against potential existential crises and thoughts of death (Sedikides and Wildschut, 2018). It seems fitting that we are turning more and more to this comfort when people have experienced . . . well the last couple years' worth of global stressors and incidents.

But, how do we choose these beloved, nostalgic characters? Do we stick to the media that was released during our childhood? Is it what our parents share with us? In 2017 we began to ask each other these questions and formulate our thoughts. Between us, we noted subtle differences in preferences as well as in the clusters of shows we held onto. Britani, a child of the '90s, April a child of the '80s, and well Keith won't answer this (we think he just may be eternal . . .) all came up with clusters of different favorites. Be it Nickelodeon, Disney, or Hanna-Barbera, each of us spoke of different icons. It made us question the idea of generational differences in regard to nostalgic cartoon shows.

The authors are aware that there are different years often associated with each of the following generations, but the dates we included appear to have the most consensus around them. We allowed participants to pick the generation in which they personally identify as being a member of for this study due to this concern. With that in mind, we classify the "Silent Generation" as those born before the 1940s, the "Baby Boomers" as those born in the early 1940s through 1960s, "Generation X" as those born in the early 1960s through the 1980s, "Millennials" as the early 1980s through the mid-1990s, and "Generation Z or Zoomers" as mid-1990s through the 2000s (Dimock, 2019). We did not include Generation Alpha as those in that generation would be too young to participate in a psychological study, as we require all participants to be at least 18 years old.

All participants were presented with the Big Five Inventory (John and Srivastava, 1999); each of the three components of the Dark Triad (with Machiavellianism as measured by the MACH-IV (Yetişer, 2014), psychopathy as measured by the SRP-III (Paulhus, Neumann, and Hare, 2009), and narcissism as measured by the NPI (Raskin and Hall, 1981)),); demographics (including information about which generation that they identified belonging to—see appendix A for a discussion on this); and over 640 popular animated characters and shows from the last 50 plus years (see appendix B for a small-ish sample of these). This was the first break from our usual survey questionnaire style. We asked participants to first rate each show on a scale of one to seven as to the degree to which they "liked" the show (1 = Strongly dislike while 7 = Strongly like). We did allow for individuals to not rate shows that they did not know. This served two purposes. First, it prevented show ratings from being skewed. Secondly, because of the very large number of shows and characters, it allowed us to use skip logic. If someone identified that they were familiar with a show by rating it, they were then asked to rate how much they "liked" the characters from that show (1 = Strongly dislike while 7 = Strongly like). If they were not familiar with the show, they were not presented with the character list and they were then presented with the next show on the list. These authors do acknowledge that it is possible to be familiar with a character but not a show, but that would have meant that everyone would have needed to go through the entire list. Based on feedback from some of our longer surveys (which are still shorter than this survey), we were worried about fatigue effects. In our cost/benefit discussion, we decided that this would be the best procedure, for now. We were grateful for the options in Qualtrics (http://www.qualtrics.com) (Qualtrics, Provo, UT) that allow us to better tailor our studies for ourselves and our participants (and ultimately for our readers).

A total of 299 individuals completed the initial survey (it is important to note that we are, as of the publishing of this chapter, still collecting data for this project partially because of the "Great Pause" that resulted from the COVID-19 pandemic). Of these, 44 percent identified as male, 55 percent identified as female, and .7 percent identified as one of the "other" options that we provided. While these demographics are fairly on par with our previous studies, this does represent a larger proportion of male respondents than is typical. Most identified as heterosexual (84.67 percent), but we did have good LGBTQIA+ identification with this smaller sample size (1.33 percent identified as gay or lesbian, 12 percent identified as bisexual, and 1.33 percent identified as "other"). We sourced most of our shows and characters from five major sources (Disney, Cartoon Network, Warner Brothers, Hanna-Barbera, and Nickelodeon), and we asked participants of which they were most a "fan." Cartoon Network led the pack with 28.09 percent, followed by Disney (25.42 percent), Warner Brothers (16.72 percent), Nickelodeon (16.39 percent), Other (7.02 percent), and, finally, Hanna-Barbera (6.35 percent).

As we mentioned previously, we also asked participants to self-identify as a member of generation they most identify with as to belonging. As previously discussed in this chapter, we realize that different sources endorse conflicting start and end dates for each of the various generations. Since we were asking participants to self-identify, we were very lenient with our dates. Our largest self-identified group was the Generation Y—Millennial—group (birth year early 1980s to mid-1990s) with 48.49 percent. This was followed by Generation X—we are too overlooked to have an interesting name and, yes, Keith and April are bitter about this—with 28.43 percent (birth year early 1960s to early 1980s), Generation Z—Zoomers—with 13.04 percent (birth year mid-1990s to mid-2000s and important to note that much of this generation does not meet the 18+ age category to participate in our surveys), and Generation W—Baby Boomers—with 10.03 percent (birth year early 1940s to early 1960s). We thought that we would find some statistically significant differences between preferences for shows or sources based on generation. For example, we hypothesized that a show like *The Flintstones* (Reed, Blanc, Vander Pyl, Benaderet, and Stephenson, 2008), which was first aired in the 1960s, would be most nostalgic, and hence most popular, with those who would have watched it as children (either Baby Boomers or Gen Xers). However, there were no significant differences demonstrated, for this or other shows, based on self-identified generation. Given the popularity of many of these shows, they have been replayed in syndication, rebooted, or re-adapted. This seems to transcend the time for which they were developed.

Our most liked shows, in order, were: *Looney Tunes, Scooby-Doo, Tom and Jerry, Jetsons, Futurama, Animaniacs, Darkwing Duck, The Flintstones, TaleSpin,* and *Tiny Toon Adventures.* Our least liked shows, in order, were: *G.I. Joe, Thundercats, Ed, Edd, n Eddy, South Park, Johnny Test, Ren & Stimpy, Kim Possible, Proud Family, Adventures of the Gummi Bears,* and *Mighty B.* Please keep in mind that these were only rated by individuals who were familiar with the shows, and to rate how much participants liked individual characters, they had to first endorse knowing the show. Our most liked characters, in order, were: Scooby-Doo, Dino (*The Flintstones*), Bugs Bunny (*Looney Tunes*), Wile E. Coyote (*Looney Tunes*), Darkwing Duck (*Disney*), Tweety Bird (*Looney Tunes*), Bam-Bam Rubble (*The Flintstones*), Road Runner (*Looney Toons*), Jerry (*Tom and Jerry*), and Pebbles Flintstone (*The Flintstones*). Our least liked characters, in order, were: Lucy Van Pelt (*Peanuts*), Dr. Drakken (*Kim Possible*), Rerun Van Pelt (*Peanuts*), Snake Eyes (*G.I. Joe*), Rancid Rabbit (*CatDog*), Roadblock (*G.I. Joe*), Chris Griffin (*Family Guy*), Vicky the Babysitter (*Fairly Odd Parents*), MoJo JoJo (*Powerpuff Girls*), and Hawk (*G.I. Joe*).

All exploratory stepwise regression analyses were completed examining all eight sub-components of personality. As always, a Bonferroni correction was conducted to counter the number of analyses conducted and to protect our Type I error rate; the significance level has been lowered from $p < .05$ to $p < .005$ to determine significance.

In terms of our most liked shows, the majority of these, with one exception (*The Flintstones*—which was associated with lower levels of neuroticism and higher levels of Machiavellianism), were associated with higher levels of liking and higher levels of openness. These included *Looney Tunes, Tiny Toon Adventures, Pinky & the Brain, Animaniacs* (which was also predicted by lower levels of agreeableness and narcissism), *Scooby-Doo,* and *Darkwing*

Duck (which were both also predicted by higher levels of Machiavellianism), and *Futurama* (which was also predicted by higher levels of psychopathy).

Interestingly, several of the least liked shows followed the same patterns. *Ed, Edd, n Eddy*, *South Park*, *Johnny Test*, and *Ren & Stimpy* were all predicted by higher scores on both openness and psychopathy, and liking the *Mighty B* was predicted by higher scores on openness, psychopathy, and extraversion (if you have never watched the *Mighty B*—she is a little "extra"). Higher liking scores were predicted for *Kim Possible*, *The Proud Family*, and the *Adventures of the Gummi Bears* based on higher Machiavellianism scores. *G.I. Joe* and *Thundercats* were also predicted by higher scores on Machiavellianism along with higher scores on narcissism or extraversion, respectively. In short, liking the least liked shows was usually associated with openness and some aspect of the Dark Triad while liking a show that is most liked is usually just associated with openness. It is of little surprise that Machiavellianism is associated with both. As we saw in chapter 7, it is the least likely to be correlated with other measures (like attitudes toward women) that do correlate with narcissism and psychopathy.

Taking this trip down memory lane was a lot of fun. Keith and April especially enjoyed asking Britani to locate and name all Care Bears and Care Bear Cousins on our lists, and we were all excited and/or disappointed to see some of our favorites either liked or not. Keith mourned the exclusion of his beloved Disney from the most liked list, perhaps most of all (and April secretly reveled in this because in her humble opinion Disney really does ruin everything and has been the bane of her statistical analyses since the "Great Event of 2016"). That did bring up an interesting "discussion" between the three authors . . . maybe it was time to explore our favorite fandoms and what makes them our favorites.

REFERENCES

1millionmoms [@1millionmoms]. (n.d.) Tweets [Twitter profile]. Retrieved August 16, 2020, from https://twitter.com/1milmoms.

Arriaga, X., and Agnew, C. (2001). Being committed: Affective, cognitive, and conative components of relationship commitment. *Personality and Social Psychology Bulletin, 27*(9), 1190–1203.

Branch, S., Wilson, K., and Agnew, C. (2013). Committed to Oprah, Homer, or House: Using the investment model to understand parasocial relationships. *Psychology of Popular Media Culture, 2*(2), 96–109.

Danesi, M. (2012). *Introductory perspectives on popular culture: Second edition.* Lanham, MD: The Rowman & Littlefield Publishers, Inc.

Derrick, J., Gabriel, S., and Hugenberg, K. (2009). Social surrogacy: How favored television programs provide the experience of belonging. *Journal of Experimental Social Psychology, 45,* 352–362.

Dimock, M. (2019). Defining generations: Where millennials end and generation z begins. Pew Research Center. Retrieved from: https://www.pewresearch.org/fact-tank/2019/01/17/where-millennials-end-and-generation-z-begins/.

Fisher, M. and Salmon, C. (2012). Human nature and pop culture. *Review of General Psychology, 16*(2), 104–108.

Giles, D. (2002). Parasocial interaction: A review of the literature and a model for future research. *Media Psychology, 4,* 279–305.

Greenwood, D. (2009). Psychological predictors of media involvement: Solitude experiences and the need to belong. *Communication Research, 36*(5), 637–654.

Hesley, J. W., and Hesley, J. G. (1998). *Rent two films and let's talk in the morning: Second edition.* Hoboken, NJ: John Wiley & Sons, Inc.

Horton, D. and Wohl, R. (1956). Mass communication and parasocial interaction: Observations on intimacy at a distance. *Psychiatry, 19,* 215–29.

Meyers, S. (2020). *Midnight Sun.* New York: Little, Brown, and Company.

Meyers, S. (2011). *Twilight.* New York: Little, Brown, and Company.

Moyer-Guse, E., and Nabi, R. (2010). Explaining the effects of narrative in an entertainment television program: Overcoming resistance to persuasion. *Human Communication Research, 36,* 26–52.

Nan, X. (2011). Influence of television on viewing and sensation seeking on adolescents' unrealistic perceptions about smoking and smokers: Evidence from a national survey. *Mass Communication and Society, 14,* 643–665.

John, O. P., and Srivastava, S. (1999). The Big-Five trait taxonomy: History, measurement, and theoretical perspectives. In L. A. Pervin and O. P. John (Eds.)., *Handbook of personality: Theory and research* (Vol. 2, pp. 102–138). New York: Guilford Press.

Keller, P. (2020, Feb. 27). Christian hate group is now accusing Disney of indoctrinating children with the 'LGB+ agenda.' Pink News Co. Retrieved from: https://www.pinknews.co.uk/2020/02/27/one-million-moms-american-family-association-onward-disney-gay-character-lena-waithe/.

Paulhus, D. L., Neumann, C. S., and Hare, R. D. (2009). *Manual for the Self-Report Psychopathy scale.* Toronto: Multi-Health Systems.

Qualtrics software, Version XM of Qualtrics. Copyright © 2018 Qualtrics. Qualtrics and all other Qualtrics product or service names are registered trademarks or trademarks of Qualtrics, Provo, UT, USA. (http://www.qualtrics.com).

Raskin, R. N., and Hall, C. S. (1981). The Narcissistic Personality Inventory: Alternative form reliability and further evidence of construct validity. *Journal of Personality Assessment, 45,* 159–160.

Reed, A., Blanc, M., Vander Pyl, J., Benaderet, B., Stephenson, J., Hanna-Barbera Productions., & LC Purchase Collection (Library of Congress). (2008). *The Flintstones: The complete series.* Burbank, CA: Warner Home Video.

Russell, C., and Russell, D. (2009). Alcohol messages in prime-time television series. *The Journal of Consumer Affairs, 43*(1), 108–128.

Sedikides, C., and Wildschut, T. (2018). Finding meaning in nostalgia. *Review of General Psychology, 22*(1), 48–61.

Shrum, L. J. (1999). Television and persuasion: Effects of the programs between the ads. *Psychology & Marketing, 16*(2), 119–140.

Yetişer, B. (2014). Do all roads lead to Rome? The moderating role of culture and age in predicting construal level on Machiavellianism. *Journal of Yasar University, 9*(36), 6328–6337.

Chapter Nine

The Fandom of Disney

(aka Disney Ruins Everything)

So . . . 2016 brought changes that we have continued to deal with since, and no, we do not just mean politically and socially speaking (see previous chapters for those). That year we started to branch out and add different characters and options to our studies. Mainly, we added Disney characters. At the time, we were not considering them as their own designated, separate entity. We just added new characters . . . like always. We had been doing that for years! What could go wrong? Well . . . apparently a lot.

This new addition of a few characters here and there brought about changes. We started to see shifts and how, in essence, things clustered and changed between groups of characters. We saw differences in Disney versus, well, everything else during that study. But we are getting ahead of ourselves. Let's hold off on sharing those results and get to the point. To be more succinct, we saw differences in "fandoms," something we had not formally looked at in our previous studies. Fandom was, leading up to this point, something much more peripheral, not something we solely focused on in our research; but it has been a huge part of popular culture for a long time and has only grown over the years.

The term "fandom" has been brought into the popular lexicon. It refers to socio-cultural phenomena made up of a self-selected group of people who are fans of a particular person, fictional series, music, team, or other media (Lexico.com, n.d.). In the past, fandoms have been associated with excessive and obsessive fanatics (Jenson, 2002). While the terms may still hold some of this connotation, today a fandom is often considered to be a group of enthusiastic fans who are passionate about an aspect of our culture rather than something deviant. Fandom may actually be the new form of, or term for, "nostalgia," offering up those feel-good emotions and sense of longing for that devoted fan base.

As the mindsets and opinions move away from the notion that fandom is solely obsessive or excessive in nature, it has shifted toward the idea of connectivity and well-being. In fact, Vinney, Dill-Shackleford, Plante, and Bartsch (2019) posit that fandom contains dimensions and aspects related to not only fan enthusiasm and appreciation, but also social interactions. With the development of the Fan Identity Scale (FIS), they note how fans form connections with others in the fandom, be it friends in-person or via the Internet. It is passion, but it is also more than that. Fandoms give opportunities for socialization (to those who have been to a fan convention . . . you know this all too well) as well as for personal growth.

Stanfill (2019) mentions other positive aspects of fandoms. For example, fans may go online and write reviews, blogs, or just share their opinion about the latest video game or television episode. This may feel empowering to them and bring about a sense of importance (e.g., someone would take note, read, and even potentially comment on something I said!). At the same time, he proposes a more jaded or cynical viewpoint, suggesting that the media and video game industry may take advantage of these fandoms. They may incite, enthuse, or circumvent a fan base. We can see this with how some show runners will build up media attention around a character that fans love, with promises and teases that the character will have a fantastic arc in the upcoming season of a show. However, when it comes time for things to air, that character ultimately has little screen time or attention. Stanfill goes on to suggest that these industries may even try to cultivate a fan base in order to control them and make them more useful to obtain media attention, renewals, promote themselves, or help push forward some agenda.

All of this suggests that fandoms continue to grow and expand in nature. When we typically think of fandoms, they are associated with a celebrity, television show, or movie franchise. As times have changed, and there are more media outlets than just television, radio, or magazines, so have the fandoms. Booth (2015) describes how there are not only fandoms for memes (yes, we all loved Grumpy Cat), there are extensions to "universes" with fan-made episodes and spin-offs, elaborate and quite impressive cosplayers (yes, we are still impressed with the Deadpool cosplayer who asked us a question at Comic-Con International as mentioned in our preface), and there are even pornographic parodies of popular franchises (you can go watch a *Power Rangers* porn parody called *Mighty Bare Ass Power Rangers* or watch *Star Whores* instead of *Star Wars*, or *That 70's Ho* instead of *That 70's Show*).

Fandoms are their own things, which we had been seeing in a lot of ways without realizing it as trends within fandoms can wax and wane and ebb and flow as particular properties rise and fall in popularity. Click (2017) describes this occurrence in multiple different fandoms and the cyclical nature that inevitably occurs. Of course, there are the long-term, die-hard fans, but the fair-weather fans are much more the norm. Bielby and Harrington (2017) go on to discuss how fandoms fade away because of natural endings. Celebrities die, film franchises run out of stories, an actor decides to no longer work on a TV show, comics get canceled, or an author decides that she is no longer going to continue writing about a character. This can create a sense of loss, not only of the franchise or character but of the social engagement such as online forums that occur with other fans, watercooler chats with coworkers over the latest episode twist, and the ending of events such as conventions where people can come together to celebrate the fandom. The absence of these fandoms is not unlike a death or other experience that involves mourning. The difference, however, is that these losses typically go unacknowledged in other realms of the person's life.

We have seen the losses and the changes in our research and presentations without truly giving it the attention it deserved. Over the years we have collected data and watched as participants in our studies and audience members in our presentations move from excitement to ambivalence to sometimes even hatred of a particular property or set of characters and then back to excitement again. This has been clearly seen over the years in our research and collection of data related to the *Twilight Saga* and more recently the *Harry Potter* series. What was once popular now brings groans and moans from audience members when we mention them in our talks and does not feature as highly on our lists.

As stated in our previous chapters, things have grown in popularity, like YouTube, and replaced other moguls. Pop culture idols and brands come and go. However, there are some fandoms that seem to be able to stand the test of time; one in particular seemed to stick out to us. *Disney*. The juggernaut itself . . . which has devoted fans continuing to support it for over 90 years. Disney holds quite a bit of nostalgia for people and has almost become a rite of passage. It is not unusual for people with young children to be asked, "When are you taking (insert the child's name) to Disney?" Likewise, many adults will reminisce and talk about that first trip to a Disney park.

We began to wonder if there might be certain personality types that influence being a member of a fandom. Are there certain psychological aspects that impact fandoms? We also wondered if there are factors related to how strongly one might identify with a particular fandom. We decided to start with Disney since it does seem to be the biggest (they own "everything"), and it seemed to take over our research results with the outcome of Keith being thrilled, Britani trying to stay neutral, and April being annoyed.

So that brings us to what we refer to, and have mentioned a few times in previous chapters, as the "Great Event of 2016." Sigh . . . after several years of "discussion" we finally started adding Disney animation to our surveys. For the most part, our lists of favorites up to that point had been fairly consistent. We saw some movement of characters either up or down our list based on movie releases or comic plots, but they remained true to what we had come to view as popular. Think Batman (*DC Universe*), Spider-Man (*Marvel Universe*), Han Solo (*Star Wars*), and Wolverine (*Marvel Universe*) with the interesting note that the only female character that consistently made our list was Katniss Everdeen (coming off the popularity of *The Hunger Games*; Collins, 2008). Those lists changed dramatically when we added the Disney animated characters. The most liked characters on our 2016 list, in order, were: Nemo, Woody, Spider-Man/Peter Parker, Mickey Mouse, Ariel, Winnie the Pooh, Aladdin, Peter Pan, Belle, and Batman/Bruce Wayne. All of those characters except for Batman, and he was #10 on the list, are owned, at least in some part (yes, we are aware that Sony owns movie rights to the Spiderverse), by Disney. The variety of characters from different franchises, media formats, and companies could not compare to the popularity of the Disney brand when Disney characters were added into the mix.

That list has changed, and changed again, over the years as we branched out to include other fandoms and characters on our lists (especially when we added other nostalgic cartoons, as can be seen in chapter 8), as well as when we take Disney out of the mix and look at it separately. We have seen some fandoms go from dominating our most hated list to the point of needing to exclude it from analyses (looking at you, *Twilight*) to the announcement that a once popular franchise has been given a sequel, made into a TV show, or has a reboot in the works (again, looking at you, *Twilight,* which has been picked back up as *Midnight Sun* [Meyers, 2006; Meyers, 2020]). In short, fandoms are a thing. A powerful thing.

For the Disney-focused study, all participants were presented with the Big Five Inventory (John and Srivastava, 1999), demographics (including information about which generation that they identified belonging to), the 24-item (four-item subscales) Love Attitudes Scale Short Form (LAS: SF) (Hendrick, Hendrick, and Dicke, 1998), and over 150 popular characters from Disney animation. See appendix D for a sample of our "Disney" characters as we discuss the "fandoms" lists we have been developing since 2016 when we started this specific endeavor. We asked participants to rate each character on a scale of one to seven as to the degree to which they "liked" the show (1 = Strongly dislike while 7 = Strongly like). We did allow for individuals to not rate characters that they did not know. This prevented a character's ratings from being skewed.

A total of over 1500 individuals have completed some variation of the survey since its inception in 2016, but we have chosen to discuss only one of those studies since its only focus was Disney. Qualtrics (http://www .qualtrics.com) (Qualtrics, Provo, UT) was utilized to collect data and survey our participants. This study was completed in 2018 with a sample size of 477. Of these, 42 percent identified as male, 57 percent identified as female, and 1 percent identified as one of the "other" options that we provided. A full 83 percent of respondents identified as a Disney fan. The top rated characters were, in order: Genie (*Aladdin*), Simba (*Lion King*), Woody (*Toy Story*), Sulley (*Monsters Inc*), Wall-E (*Wall-E*), Edna (*The Incredibles*), Mulan (*Mulan*), Mike Wazowski (*Monsters Inc*), Tigger (*Winnie the Pooh*), and Moana (*Moana*). Much like our pre-2016 lists, this list represents some characters that seem to be relatively stable in terms of popularity (Woody, for example) but also characters that represent current movie and television trends (Moana, for example, which came out in theaters in 2016 when the "Great Event" happened).

All exploratory stepwise regression analyses were completed examining all five sub-scales of the BFI personality measure. As was reported in chapter 5, the Love Attitudes Scale Short Form (LAS: SF) (Hendrick, Hendrick, and Dicke, 1998) was used to explore the relationships between love and character shipping, but they were also used in these analyses to explore the relationships between love, personality, and how they can be used to predict which characters that we like. As always, a Bonferroni correction was used to counter the number of analyses conducted and to protect our Type I error rate; the significance level has been lowered from $p < .05$ to $p < .005$ to determine significance.

Results demonstrated relationships between only three types of love: Agape, Pragma, and Ludus/Ludos. Agape, or selfless love, was associated with: Beast (*Beauty and the Beast*) (higher levels of agreeableness and Agape predicted higher levels of liking for Beast), Nemo (*Finding Nemo*) (higher levels of agreeableness, Agape, and extraversion were more predictive of higher levels of liking Nemo), Joy (*Inside Out*) (higher levels of agreeableness, Agape, neuroticism, and extraversion were associated with more liking), Riley Anderson (*Inside Out*) (higher levels of Agape and neuroticism were associated with more liking), and Anger[1] (*Inside Out*) (higher levels of Agape and lower levels of Pragma were associated with more liking). It is very interesting that three separate characters (all emotion and self-based) were predicted by self-less love.

Four characters were associated with Pragma (the practical, convenience-based love style). Aladdin (*Aladdin*) was predicted to be more liked by those scoring higher on agreeableness, neuroticism, and Pragma. Maleficent (*Sleeping Beauty*) was more liked by those endorsing higher levels of both

Pragma and extraversion. Higher levels of openness and Pragma predicted more liking of Mr. Incredible[2] (*The Incredibles*), and Prince Charming (*Cinderella*) was associated with higher levels of conscientiousness and Pragma.

Quite possibly the most interesting results (and the only reason that April agreed to write the results for this chapter) were for Ludus/Ludos (love as a conquest). There was a definite and concrete theme to all the characters that exhibited a relationship with Ludus/Ludos. All of the characters, except for one, were more liked by those exhibiting higher levels of both extra version and Ludus/Ludos. They were Cruella De Vil (*101 Dalmatians*), Gaston (*Beauty and the Beast*), Jafar (*Aladdin*), Lady Tremain/Wicked Stepmother (*Cinderella*), Mother Gothel (*Tangled*), Queen of Hearts (*Alice in Wonderland*), Scar (*The Lion King*), Shere Khan (*The Jungle Book*), Evil Queen (*Snow White*) (who was also associated with lower levels of agreeableness), Tinker Bell (*Peter Pan*) (who was also associated with higher levels of agreeableness—and for those of you thinking that Tinker Bell is the helpful fairy—she is also very jealous and a bit mean-spirited toward Wendy [Barrie, 1904]), and Ursula (*The Little Mermaid*) (who was also associated with higher levels of openness). The only exception was Hans (*Frozen*), who was associated with higher levels of Ludus/Ludos but instead of extraversion, liking him was also associated with lower levels of neuroticism. Hans, unlike all the others, seems to be a little more hesitant and waits to tell you his evil plans (Vecho [Producer], 2013).

So, Disney . . . is its own thing. Just as we see fandoms as their own thing. These studies, much to April's annoyance, turned the corner in how we viewed our character lists and how we approached delving into the various corners of popular culture. In some ways, it is not just about the characters we love, and hate, and love to hate. It is about the fandoms and the meaning that they give us. Be it Disney and the nostalgia it brings up for its diehard fans, or the fandoms we have not even yet explored (*Supernatural, Doctor Who, Star Trek*, etc.), fandoms are something special.

Furthermore, with Disney acquiring Pixar, Star Wars, Marvel, and Fox, it has only solidified its hold on fandoms in the future. This continues in every branch of Disney's properties from merchandise to media releases, to walking into a Disney park and all of your fandoms being present in one interactive location (a true vacation destination). And despite what April may think about Disney, a member of one of these fandoms (Keith, we are looking at you) would grab his Mouse ears and gleefully say that Disney will truly be (if it already isn't for you), the "Happiest Place on Earth."

NOTES

1. These characters were only marginally significant. They met the $p < .05$ benchmark but not the $p < .005$ benchmark.

2. See note 1.

REFERENCES

Barrie, J. M. (1904). *Peter Pan* [Play]. London.

Bielby, D., and Harrington, C. L. (2017). The lives of fandoms. In Gray J., Sandvoss, C., and Harrington C. L. (Eds.), *Fandom, Second Edition: Identities and Communities in a Mediated World* (pp. 205–221). New York: NYU Press.

Booth, P. (2015). *Playing fans: Negotiating fandom and media in the digital age.* Iowa City, IA: University of Iowa Press.

Buck, C., and Lee, J. (Directors). (2013). *Frozen.* [Motion Picture]. Burbank, California: Walt Disney Pictures.

Click, M. A. (2017). Do all "good things" come to an end?: Revisiting Martha Stewart fans after ImClone. In Gray, J., Sandvoss, C., and Harrington, C. L. (Eds.), *Fandom, Second Edition: Identities and Communities in a Mediated World* (pp. 191–204). New York: NYU Press.

Collins, S. (2008). *The Hunger Games.* New York: Scholastic Press.

Hendrick, C., Hendrick, S. S., and Dicke, A. (1998) The Love Attitudes Scale: Short Form. *Journal of Social and Personal Relationships, 15*(2), 147–159.

Jenson, J. (2002). Fandom as pathology: The consequences of characterization. In L. A. Lewis (Ed.), *Adoring Audience: Fan Culture and Popular Media* pp. 9–26 New York, NY: Routledge.

John, O. P., and Srivastava, S. (1999). The Big-Five trait taxonomy: History, measurement, and theoretical perspectives. In L. A. Pervin and O. P. John (Eds.). *Handbook of personality: Theory and research* (Vol. 2, pp. 102–138). New York: Guilford Press.

Lexico. (n.d.). Definition of fandom in English. Retrieved from: https://www.lexico.com/en/definition/fandom.

Meyers, S. (2020). *Midnight Sun.* New York: Little Brown.

Meyers, S. (2006). *New Moon.* New York: Little Brown.

Qualtrics software, Version XM of Qualtrics. Copyright © 2018 Qualtrics. Qualtrics and all other Qualtrics product or service names are registered trademarks or trademarks of Qualtrics, Provo, UT, USA. (http://www.qualtrics.com).

Stanfill, M. (2019). *Exploiting fandom: How the media industry seeks to manipulate fans.* Iowa City, IA: University of Iowa Press.

Vinney, C., Dill-Shackleford, K. E., Plante, C. N., and Bartsch, A. (2019, March 21). Development and validation of a measure of popular media fan identity and its relationship to well-being. *Psychology of Popular Media Culture.* Advance online publication.

Chapter Ten

Conclusions and Future Directions

With popular shows such as the *Big Bang Theory* and blockbuster movies such as *The Avengers*, being called a "nerd" is no longer seen as a bad thing. Just as fandoms and characters wax and wane, the concept of "nerd" has also changed. What was once an insult is now a title that many proudly claim. These pop culture characters have made being a "nerd" so mainstream that many fans would not even consider themselves "nerds" because the characters are popular, normalized, liked, and we can identify with them. If they do adopt the self-concept of "nerd" it is now usually done with pride.

Pop culture has always and continues to play a significant role in our modern society. It is not unusual for people to wear apparel with their favorite superhero or pop culture character. Pop culture-themed merchandise can be easily found in just about any store. In fact, there are even stores that have turned pop culture into their brand. People don't think twice about someone walking down the street wearing a shirt with Mickey Mouse (*Disney*) on it or a baseball cap with the Legend of Zelda (*Nintendo*) symbol embroidered on it. We have a president of the United States (Donald Trump) campaign superimposing his head on Thanos's (*Marvel Universe*) body, ready to engage in "the snap" to former President Barak Obama in the *Amazing Spider-Man* #583 comic (*Marvel Universe*) (for more on these, see chapter 4). Social media posts flood the Internet from celebrities talking about their comic-related projects to movie studios promoting their next blockbuster. With crises such as the 9/11 terrorist attacks and the COVID-19 pandemic, we see images of our favorite superheroes saluting and showing respect to the front-line workers. These images demonstrate these fictional characters respecting and identifying who the true heroes are in our world.

Not only is there a societal impact from these pop culture characters, but there is an emotional impact as well. This emotional impact can be seen with fans "up in arms" over the series finale of *The Sopranos* (or *Game of Thrones*) to fans sending television networks crates of fake bananas in support of *Arrested Development* (Oswald, 2018). If we have demonstrated nothing else from our research, we have shown over and over that people love these characters, "ship" them, are devoted to them, and even 'stan them. Pop culture speaks to those who want and need to be seen. From the X-Men mutants (*Marvel Universe*) being associated with the civil rights movement and the LGBTQIA+ population to Kamala Khan (aka Miss Marvel [*Marvel Universe*]) being the first Muslim superhero to Freddy Freeman (aka Captain Marvel, Jr. [*DC Universe*]) who is physically challenged, these characters are important for representation of the world that we live in (please see chapter 8 for more on this). They normalize the things that need normalized, and they speak for the populations who have no voice.

Nevins (2017) discusses how the concept of superheroes continues to develop and change over time. From as far back as the Greek gods such as Zeus, these characters speak to us, we identify with them, we learn from them, and even grow from the lessons and adventures that they convey in their tales. We see them illustrated and exemplified in everything from Egyptian poems, to our Biblical heroes, to medieval epics, to Elizabethan urban legends, to Gothic novels, to dime-store comics, and to pulp magazines. These archetypes have remained relevant, powerful, and popular.

One of the reasons why these have been maintained in our societies in various iterations has to do with the fact that these characters teach us lessons about life and the difference between good and bad. There are children's books based on *DC Universe* characters that have Superman demonstrating how to be respectful in the story (Harbo and Frampton, 2018), Wonder Woman being helpful to others in her book (Harbo and Frampton, 2018), and the Flash engaging in generosity in his adventure (Harbo, Lokus, and Schigiel, 2019). They are modern-day fables and lessons on striving to be a better person even when the odds are against us. These characters inspire us—they inspire me.

Our research has shown us that there is evidence that there are individual personality traits that are associated with pop culture preferences. We have more evidence for what pop culture trends rise and fall and potential factors that impact those trends. But after nearly a decade of researching pop culture and human factors, what is perhaps the most powerful thing that we have learned? We have learned that we have only begun to scratch the surface of what we can discover.

The importance of popular culture and the need to understand it continues to excite us, and the research that we have conducted and discussed in this book only serves to further drive and support those things that we have always loved. We hope it excites you too, and you can see that not only is pop culture something we enjoy, but research is something that can be fun too. Never once during that first conversation between Keith and April about potentially collaborating on a study about superheroes, did we think we would end up here. It has been an adventure, similar to those that we avidly read about in the pages of our favorite comic. And, just like the never-ending tales that we enjoy, so is our research a never-ending adventure.

We have also been inspired to look at new topics and areas of pop culture because of *YOU*. Through questions audience members have asked when we have presented our research at various conventions, to media outlets contacting us for interviews, and even interested individuals who get in touch with us just to chat, we have new ideas and topic areas that we want to explore. As a result, our research continues and grows in multiple different directions.

For a couple of professors who began talking about pop culture over the watercooler a decade ago (and one student turned instructor), maybe the biggest new direction that our research has taken is in the classroom. Keith has taught a course (writing intensive, no less) on the Psychology of Superheroes. April added the Psychology of Pop Culture as a formal course to the Marshall University course catalog and has regularly team taught such classes as The Psychology of Stephen King and the Psychology of the Apocalypse (that one is particularly handy as we close out writing and editing this book—although nothing we have taught covered toilet paper shortages). Britani and April have also been fortunate enough to teach several Honors courses centered on pop culture. One of our favorites (directly related to the content of chapter 3) was The Heroes and Villains of Healthcare, and our newest one (to be taught again in Fall 2020) is simply called Internet Famous and explores the psychological and social aspects that have made YouTube and other online media personalities famous and created multi-million dollar franchises. We love our students, and we love our classes and the opportunities that bring us to continue this work.

Some readers of this text might be wondering what we could possibly be teaching in these courses that would be important enough to warrant them being in the academic catalog. Fun, certainly, but what might these pop culture issues be covering that is so very terribly important? Well . . . turns out a hell of a lot. First of all, chapter 4 tells us that these questions about the relevancy of pop culture research are much more likely to originate from our more conservative friends (who are also much less likely to be reading this book, in the first place). Chapter 6 goes on to tell us that these same individuals, or rather individuals that hold these ideas, are far more likely to be Internet trolls. And we know that Internet trolls are much more likely to be the ones making life miserable for women (chapter 7), individuals in the LGBTQIA+ community (chapter 5), and minorities (chapter 4), in general. Now, to be absolutely clear, none of the authors of this book would pretend for even a moment that individuals (broadly speaking) who identify as conservative would hold these views (correlation is not causation, and we would *NEVER* pretend that it is), but we do know that more individuals who identify with fewer pro-feminist views, more negative views toward minorities, and more trolling behavior do tend to identify as conservative.

As educators, we tend to believe that with a little education, we can counter these ideas. Education gives us the power to open minds and broaden perspectives and sneak in those statements about correlation not being causation but being careful because the association . . . the relationship is still there. A lot of those ideas and topics are much easier to address with pop culture as the basis for exploring them. The sheer accessibility and reach of pop culture make it the perfect conduit to educate, so we do. How, you ask?

Here is one of April's favorite tricky approaches at some metacognition (thinking about our own thinking).

April—I use this in a couple of my undergraduate courses (including in my Introduction to Psychology and Psychology of Popular Culture courses). At the very beginning of the class, I open up YouTube and play the video for the song *Do You Feel It* from Chaos Chaos (Weisenhaus and Weisenhaus, 2014) (Rick and Morty, 2017) to then showing a clip of Season 2, Episode 3 of *Rick and Morty* where Rick seemingly has a failed suicide attempt (Ridley and Newton, 2015). Suicide is always a difficult topic. Almost an impossible topic, but it is also an important topic. Especially to freshmen who are far from home for the first time and scared and afraid and worried about failing. Losing a student, for any reason, is painful; but losing one to suicide as someone from the psychology field is heartbreaking in a particularly hellish sort of way. This video . . . this cartoon . . . gives me a chance to start that conversation. I get to share the Suicide Prevention Lifeline (www.suicidepreventionlifeline.org) at 1-800-273-8255, and I get to share The Trevor Project (www.thetrevorproject. org) for the TrevorLifeline at 1-866-488-7386 for LGBTQIA+ community members. Likewise, I get to share university resources for these students. Most of all, I get to tell them that they matter, that I care, and that it would break me to lose a single one of them. That it would break me at the end of the lecture or 20 years from now because each and every human in that room matters that much, and there is help. An often controversial cartoon and a song . . . that gets me there. It gets them thinking. It puts an ally in the room. It creates allies in them. It is worth every moment of that lecture. I use music for addiction and movies for memory and many other "tricks" to get them talking and engaging and thinking. I hide it in the things I love. I hide it in the things they love, and whether they realize it or not, I get it to them. That is the important bit. We get it to them, and we know more, and they know more. And the research is what gets us there.

April is not the only instructor of this group to find meaning and utilize popular culture in the classroom. Here is Britani and one of her own personal favorite classroom experiences and examples:

Britani—I'm a "Marvel girl." Through and through . . . and not just the movies. As much as I started my obsession and my own personal fan journey with the movies, I am a fan of the comic book material. That brought me to the Matt Fraction (Fraction, Aja, and Hollingsworth, 2015) run of *Hawkeye* comics. This run includes the issues where Fraction and David Aja create a set of panels that are solely drawn using sign language. Fraction created a full story where the famed marksman loses his hearing and must default back to sign language due to his injuries. The comic is beautiful and powerful. Fraction discussed how the issue was "an opportunity for hearing people to get a taste of what it might be like to be deaf" as the issue forces the reader to rely solely on context clues to understand what is happening (as cited in Armitage, 2014). The writers and artists involved in this comic created a scenario to represent what a deaf individual may experience in a hearing world, relying on context clues and images to understand what is being said.

I was a fan, long before I was a "teacher." I fell into teaching much the same way I fell into this research. Someone (April in this case) looked at me and said "do this cool thing." And I did. I started teaching for the Honors College. It was one of the best decisions of my life. It allowed me to bring interesting, powerful popular culture to students. Students who were not psychology majors and had little understanding (in many cases) of psychological themes, topics, and research. It was in one of these classes I utilized Fraction's *Hawkeye* comic specifically. The class revolved on the use of language and alternative forms of communication, and the psychological themes that arose within this issue.

My students read *Hawkeye*. And many found themselves confused and lost trying to comprehend what the sign language drawn into the panels meant. And they got it. They got the struggle. The difficulty that relying on images and context clues can bring about. It was definitely a more powerful, meaningful lesson on ableism than I could have delivered through a lecture alone. The assignment of reading this book, of diving into the sign language of the panels, made it an immersive experience, something a lecture could not have provided. Since teaching that class for the first time, I have not looked back. Even when I am not teaching a popular culture specific course, I find meaning and ways to use it. It's a uniting force. It is powerful.

Well, Keith hates to be left out so let him discuss with you how he has used pop culture to help aid him in his teaching.

Keith—As mentioned earlier in this chapter, I taught a course on super-heroes and psychology that was writing intensive. We talk about personality theory and how/why these characters may be motivated to behave in such a way based on various psychological concepts. We also explore mental health issues that are often portrayed in comics, such as Dr. Victor Fries (aka Mr. Freeze [*DC Universe*]) dealing with bereavement over the loss of his wife (Kirkland and Rogel, 1998), The Hulk's (*Marvel Universe*) anger issues, the Minions (*Despicable Me*) who seem to suffer from Attention Deficit Hyperactivity Disorder, and the concept of masculinity and gender equality (or lack thereof) conveyed in comics. One task that the class had to do in smaller groups was to create characters and write a comic book. However, being a psychologist, I know that there is "psychology" in everything. I make them initially create a psychological profile of the characters that they create and think about how those personality aspects influence the decisions, rationality, and choices that their characters will make through the story they create. I find that the students begin to recognize the prevalence of mental health issues in their world. This may normalize their own experience or help them gain empathy for those whom they come into contact with.

My "other job" is as a therapist. There is a teaching component to that work as well. These pop culture characters are rich in lessons and guidance that they can give us. For example, I had a patient who was suffering from significant anxiety. We had been working for some time with little progress, and then she mentioned how she liked Black Widow (*Marvel Universe*). This provided me an opportunity to explore what aspects of Black Widow's personality and traits that my patient admired. She talked about her confidence, belief in herself, and determination to get a job done. We talked about putting on the "persona" or mask that was mentioned in chapter 1. She would then engage in this character's behavior to see what it was like (no, I didn't have her wear black leather or beat up people). When the patient would get into a situation that created anxiety for her, I would have her remind herself how Black Widow would act in this situation and to try on that "role" or mask in the moment. The result was the patient realizing that many of her irrational fears and concerns were just that—irrational—and with more successful experiences and interactions the "role" began to get integrated into her personality. The concept of using pop culture to aid in the treatment of mental health issues is nothing new. There are books, blogs, and websites that list various movies, shows, and characters effectively dealing with and overcoming mental health issues and how these can be integrated into treatment (Hesley and Hesley, 1998; Izod, 2006; Schwitzer and Rubin, 2014; Solomon, 2015; Sandwell, 2018).

For these reasons, and more, we continue on with our research. We currently have research exploring the 2016 presidential election (data already collected) and the current (as of the writing of this book) 2020 presidential election cycle (to compare and contrast the results) and how pop culture, personality traits such as the Dark Triad, and alignments such as "lawful good" or "chaotic evil" may go together. We are also continuing to explore specific fandoms and those that are long lasting, such as *Lord of the Rings*, *Doctor Who*, *Harry Potter*, *Star Trek*, and of course, the juggernaut of them all—*Disney*. For example, we are currently working on a study exploring the fandom of *Supernatural* and spiritual components that may be associated with those who love the show.

We are also branching out into different pop culture areas such as gaming, anime, and horror genres. Much like the Internet study in chapter 6, we have started collecting data on TikTok and the legends of pop culture themselves. Where would we be without the Elvis Presleys or Mister Rogerses of the world, and what would those iconic legends have looked like in a YouTube and TikTok world? Just the idea of ASMR Bob Ross original content alone soothes our pandemic quarantine anxiety. We are even looking at seasonal cultural factors and events that influence pop culture. For example, we are looking at personality and the popularity of Christmas music, television shows, and movies. In fact, we presented some our results for this study at the 2020 Virtual Comic-Con International at Home event.

We are also branching out in how we collect our data. With our new *Harry Potter* study, we collected data from the United States and from the United Kingdom in order to compare and contrast the results. We want to continue to research on a global scale, especially since pop culture has such a societal aspect to it. We are also expanding how we collect data, moving toward tapping into other social media platforms to help collect data on certain populations who might not typically take our surveys through our typical distribution and advertisement methods. As mentioned in a previous chapter, we initially started to collect data using Amazon MTurk but have moved away from this data collection method to using more social media platforms to advertise and sample populations of interest to us.

We have also added additional measures from when we first started this journey. In addition to the personality and interest inventories we are currently using, we have explored some alternative instruments that we are going to add to or replace what we have used. This will help us establish additional evidence for our findings and strengthen the validity and reliability of the concepts and methods that we proposed. Likewise, our pop culture character and show lists have grown. We started out with 200 characters and have "added" another zero to that number with multiple studies, select characters, shows, movies, genres, fandoms, or media platforms. In total, we are looking at over 2,000 pop culture items and adding more with every study.

So much has changed for the Con Family in the last decade. But at our core, we have remained a family. You'd be shocked if you'd seen us while writing this book. Laughter over the table while dividing and conquering only to realize that we had the same questions for each other when we came back together. Love and loss and growth have all been factors that have led us to this point. Here, as in the preface, we thought maybe it best that you hear from each of us—our voice becoming our voices.

April—A decade of research with these humans. A decade of amazing experiences. My two co-authors have shared my most amazing moments as a researcher, scientist, professor, and mother over that time. Triumphs and beautiful days and top ten moments. They have also shared my hardest days with me. Badly coded datasets and confusing results and loss . . . the real kind that breaks your heart in that impossible way that means it can never be fully mended. This research bound us, but it is the things we are researching that hold us tight. Stolen texts at midnight with *Mandalorian* memes to Britani and links to Disney merchandise over lunch meetings to Keith (he usually buys the item). We research these things because we love them. We do not always find what we hope to find, and we tease, and bicker, and we are all incredibly different, but we love each other. I love them . . . these two family members of mine, and the studies, and all the things pop culture (even Disney, except mostly just the villains). I can't wait to see what we study next. I can't wait for the next Con. And I sincerely hope we will get to share some really cool things over the next decades with you.

Britani—I don't know where to begin. A lot has happened since I started working on this. I was just a student . . . a research assistant. I said, at one point, I could never present to a room of people, and that cons and writing a book were just bucket list items. None of that felt real. But here we are. Here I am. I have done those things. I have gone from being one of the "con kids" who needed to learn how to go on an airplane for the first time to mothering the next set of researchers somehow. It's been an amazing journey, one in which I am forever grateful to these co-authors. We have become a family, and it has been a wild ride since we started. I echo the excitement for the next chapter . . . whatever that may be.

Keith—Being a clinical psychologist, I hope you will allow me to be a little more touchy-feely in my final part of this book (yes, April, if you can talk stats then I can talk about emotions). As I think back over the past decade of this research and where we are now, I actually begin to think even further back . . . to being a five-year-old boy and my mother safety-pinning a red towel around my neck so I could run around outside with my little brother (decked out in a blue safety-pinned towel) and pretending to be Superman and Batman saving the world—or at least our backyard. Don't lose that excitement for the things you love and carry them with you even when others may think that you are much too old to be interested in superheroes or Mickey Mouse. I hope I never lose that child-like spirit and feeling of excitement that comes while watching something superhero-related and the hero seems down and out and the theme music begins to slowly crescendo in the background, growing stronger as the anticipation of what happens next also grows. You know a come-back is going to happen, and it will be awesome!

As mentioned earlier, beyond being a clinical psychologist, I am also a professor. I value learning and conveying that knowledge, so I can't help but take this moment to "teach" you a little something beyond the theories, stats, results, and conclusions of our research. I would like to impart some words of wisdom related to our research journey, more so than from the research itself:

Be brave, ask questions, share your knowledge to the masses, and do things outside of your comfort zone. This research has provided me with opportunities that I never thought I would have and some experiences that few people ever have the privilege to do. Even though there have been a lot of great opportunities that have come from our research, there have been some disappointments. Be realistic in your expectations and learn to enjoy what you receive even if it isn't what you wanted or hoped for. I would not change a lot of what we have gained from this experience.

I like to tease, although there is a little truth in it, that April scares me. I am pretty sure she is the Disney villain to my Disney princess. Don't let her fool you—she loves Disney—well, it may be a love-hate relationship, but there is still some love there. I could not have started or continue to do this research without her. Work with people who know more than you. They will push you, amaze you with their skills and knowledge, challenge you to learn about things you didn't know much about, and help you discover new things that you enjoy. Additionally, work with people who don't know as much as you so you can teach them the "ways of the force," see them grow and become, in the theme of *Star Wars*, a Jedi master who will then, in turn, teach you something. Britani, who was once a student, is now a "Jedi master" in her own right and she has brought fresh ideas and has brought other pop culture areas into our research that I am less familiar with and learning more about. I have learned more from all of the student assistants who have worked with us on this research than I think I have taught them.

As we have mentioned in previous chapters, research is never perfect and there is always a chance for some error. For example, when we first made our list of pop culture characters, we left off Harry Potter. We had all the other expected *Potterverse* characters—but him. Needless to say, he has been added in. Remember, mistakes will happen, learn from them, laugh about them, fix them, and keep moving forward. I will add that even though Harry may have been missing—Batman will always be a part of our research.

Batman holds a special and unique meaning for each of us that I won't take the time to get into, but we all have that certain someone who comes into our lives, changes our life in ways that are heroic, and silently slips away into the night; and you don't even realize it until you turn around and realize he is gone. Our Batman may be off on another adventure but is forever a part of our Con Family.

Another lesson that this research journey has taught be me to be flexible. Things may not start out with the results that you expected but that doesn't mean you freak out (OK, maybe it is OK to freak out a little). The night before our first Comic-Con International presentation, we realized that the audience that we were presenting our research to was unlike our typical conference audience and scrapped most of the presentation to adjust it to better fit the audience and convey the important findings we discovered in a new way that we had never done before. So, recognize that in life you may have to change things at the last minute, and being part of a team, part of a family, part of a Con Family, sometimes means you have to change what you want or how you think things need to go so that the end result can come together in the best way possible.

Everyone has an opinion. People can say lots of things, but that doesn't make it true. Opinions have their place but what are the facts and data to back up what you say? Research allows us to be able to make the claims and conclusions that we reach based on the evidence and support for the findings. Sure, I can give you my opinion about things and so can anyone else. You have a more solid stance if you have evidence to support your position.

Additionally, being in academia, people may also have thoughts about the research that we do. We have had people say that this research isn't important or even "real" research. I say, do the research anyway. It is important to someone. It is important to me, it is important to you for whatever reason you bought this book, and you may be a superstar in someone's eyes because of the things that you have knowledge about. Remember, you are important to someone and what you do is important to others, sometimes in ways that you don't even know. Is our research going to change the world? Nah—but that doesn't mean that we shouldn't do it, contribute to the field, and convey the knowledge to others.

And my last bit of advice from this journey—always make sure you have the cords you need for presentations.

So, what have we already found in some of our newest research? What will we find in the research that we are getting ready to conduct? I guess you will just have to wait . . . for the sequel!

REFERENCES

Armitage, H. (2014, July 28). Hawkeye is deaf in Matt Fraction and David Aja's sign-language issue. Digital Spy. Retrieved from: https://www.digitalspy.com/comics/a586891/hawkeye-is-deaf-in-matt-fraction-and-david-ajas-sign-language-issue/.

Fraction, M., Aja, D., and Hollingsworth, M. (2015). *Hawkeye: Rio Bravo #19.* New York, New York: Marvel Comics.

Harbo, C., Lokus, R., and Schigiel, G. (2019). *Wonder Woman perseveres.* Picture Window Books.

Harbo, C., and Frampton, O. (2018a). *Superman is a good citizen.* Picture Window Books.

Harbo, C., and Frampton, O. (2018b). *The Flash is caring.* Picture Window Books.

Hesley, J. W., and Hesley, J. G. (1998). *Rent two films and let's talk in the morning: Second edition.* Hoboken, NJ: John Wiley & Sons, Inc.

Izod, J. (2006). *Screen, culture, psyche.* Abingdon-on-Thames, England, UK: Routledge.

Kirkland, B. (Producer and Director), and Rogel, R. (Producer). (1998). *Batman & Mr. Freeze: SubZero* [Motion Picture]. United States: Warner Bros. Pictures.

Nevins, J. (2017). *The evolution of the costumed avenger: The 4,000–year history of the superhero.* Santa Barbara, CA: ABC-CLIO, LLC.

Oswald, A. (2018, June 13). 16 times fans saved TV shows from cancellation. Insider. Retrieved from: https://www.insider.com/fans-saved-tv-show-2018-6.

Rick and Morty. (2017, October 18). *Chaos Chaos–Do You Feel It* [Video File] Retrieved from https://www.youtube.com/watch?v=jV6U7ZIPKEA.

Ridley, R. (Writer), and Newton, B. (Director). (2015, August 9). Auto Erotic Assimilation. [Television series episode]. In Roiland, J. and Harmon, D. (Creator). *Rick and Morty.* [TV program].

Sandwell, I. (2018). *The 20 best movies about mental illness that get it right.* GamesRadar +. Retrieved from https://www.gamesradar.com/best-movies-about-mental-illness/.

Schwitzer, A. M., and Rubin, L. C. (2014). *Diagnosis and treatment planning skills: A popular culture casebook approach,* 2nd ed. Los Angeles, CA: Sage.

Solomon, G. (2015). *Reel therapy: How movies inspire you to overcome life's problems.* Pennsauken, NJ: BookBaby.

Weisenhaus, A., and Weisenhaus, C. (2014). *Do You Feel It* [Recorded by Chaos Chaos: formerly Smoosh]. On Chaos Chaos [recording]. Brooklyn, NY: Independent.

Appendix A

Sample Demographics from Over the Years

Please note that these demographics are not an exhaustive list nor the exact wording of our survey questions. In fact, many of these have changed substantially over the years for a couple of reasons. First, Keith, Britani, and April are always striving to use the most inclusive language possible. That language, and our awareness of our use of language, has grown and evolved over the last 10 years. We do not always get it right. We wish that we did, and we will strive to be better . . . to grow . . . to learn more. Our surveys are constantly evolving to match pop culture changes and to embrace the amazingly diverse group of humans who consume it. In other words, these are examples of some of our items.

Secondly, "magicians" never reveal all of their secrets, especially when they are still collecting data and running studies and prepping many more very cool things to share at conventions, in our presentations, in research publications, and potential future texts. Please be patient with us. We will share . . . by now we hope you know that no one loves talking about these things more than these three nerds who have spent the last decade steeped in the science of psychology and all things pop culture. In fact, we can't wait to share with you.

Finally, since this is a composite list it applies to every chapter in this book. While we have not referenced it in every chapter (and some demographic questions are spoiler alerts), this appendix can be applied any time we are referencing the demographics for a particular study.

Sample Items:

- Gender
- Ethnicity

- Sexual Orientation*
- Marital Status
- Highest Education Level (highest degree received)
- Employment Status (primary source of income)
- Household Income (U.S. Dollars—yes, this has become problematic for at least one of our studies that we are currently working on)
- I would consider myself a fan of (select types of Internet media)
- I would consider myself a fan of (select comic and/or graphic novel publisher)
- I would consider myself a fan of pop culture in general
- I would consider myself a fan of (select fandoms—this would definitely be a spoiler alert and Keith and Britani said that I am not allowed to say anything here, but I don't actually think they always read all of my methodology and statistics stuff so I'll just say Baby Yoda—The Child [Favreau, 2019] and leave it at that)
- I would consider myself an Internet troll
- I would consider myself a fan of superhero-related genres and media
- I prefer (or identify) as belonging to House _____ (and oh yes, we know that House can reference several things)
- Which of the following do you identify as your political affiliation?
- I identify as (this question refers to religion and spirituality, and we have lots of options, but we know we have more work to do)

  - Baptist
  - Methodist
  - Anglican
  - Catholic
  - Lutheran
  - Church of God
  - Evangelical
  - Presbyterian
  - Jehovah's Witness
  - Pentecostal
  - Episcopalian
  - Mormon
  - Assembly of God
  - Churches of Christ
  - Congregational
  - Muslim
  - Atheist
  - Agnostic
  - Jewish

- ○ Buddhist
- ○ Hindu
- ○ Christian Nondenominational
- ○ Other Christian
- ○ Other

- I consider myself a member of which of the following generations (see chapter 8 for a discussion on how we know that these dates for generational membership are not completely agreed upon by everyone, and see chapter 1 for a discussion on how self-identification and psychometrically vetted measures can work together to give us convergent evidence about our participants)

  - ○ Generation Z (Post-Millennials) [Birth Year Mid-1990s to Mid-2000s]
  - ○ Generation Y (Millennials) [Birth Year Early 1980s to Mid-1990s]
  - ○ Generation X [Birth Year Early 1960s to Early 1980s]
  - ○ Baby Boomers [Birth Year Early 1940s to Early 1960s]
  - ○ Other

*Sexual orientation is one question that we have added to significantly over the years. As our understanding of the LGBTQIA+ population has grown, we have added a second question about sexual orientation based on the work of Kinsey, Pomeroy, and Martin (1948). This question asks:

On a scale of 1 to 7 (or 0 to 6), please indicate how you think about your sexuality.

0 | Exclusively heterosexual
1 | Predominantly heterosexual, only incidentally homosexual
2 | Predominantly heterosexual, but more than incidentally homosexual
3 | Equally heterosexual and homosexual
4 | Predominantly homosexual, but more than incidentally heterosexual
5 | Predominantly homosexual, only incidentally heterosexual
6 | Exclusively homosexual
7 | No socio-sexual contacts or reactions

REFERENCES

Favreau, J. (Producer). (2019). *The Mandalorian.* United States: Walt Disney Studios.
Kinsey, A. C., Pomeroy, W. B., & Martin, C. E. (1948). *Sexual Behavior in the Human Male.* Philadelphia, PA: W. B. Saunders Company.

Appendix B

Sample Characters, Superpowers, Shows, 'Ships, et cetera . . .

As with demographics, this is in no way an exhaustive list (or lists) from the last decade of research. In chapter 1, we gave a brief discussion of how our very first list was created. In short, Keith, April, and Britani all argued about what was popular at the box office, who was being talked about at the watercooler (in both positive and negative ways), and definitely all of our great loves. We were pretty proud of that list of over 200 characters. We felt pretty good about the scope. We had characters (good and bad) from a variety of movies, and TV shows, and books. Then we went to our first large convention together. There were so many MORE things represented. The wide world of fandoms and nerddom clearly left us with the knowledge that there was so much still untapped. So . . . we added things.

We added superpowers, then cable shows, and then streaming shows, and then ships, and then . . . we got trolled. Like seriously trolled. People hated our surveys. They were so long! With each list we were fighting with each other and talking to each other to make sure that we had enough representation without going "full on down the rabbit hole", but that meant we weren't deep enough and characters one of us saw as unimportant had someone else on the team arguing that the whole "world" (i.e., all aspects of their universe including people, places, and things) resulted in some feature of that character being manifested. For example, Superman might not be so "super" without Jimmy Olson (*DC Universe*) to save. Then Keith wore April down in what we refer to as the "Great Event of 2016," and we added Disney. That is when the trolling started with mean emails and social media posts. Our surveys were long, but they were not enough. There was so much more we wanted to do. We did what any good researcher does . . . we got clever with the methodology. First, we started using skip logic (see chapter 9 for a discussion on skip logic). Secondly, we started breaking the lists apart. We are collecting the same information at the same time, at any given time, on between six and ten separate lists. This takes many more participants, of course, but it does lessen the trolling a bit. Which preserves Keith's sanity, so this appendix is a sample of those lists.

Remember, this is a composite list and not a comprehensive list. It applies to every chapter in this book. While we have not referenced it in every chapter (so many spoiler alerts on this list), this appendix can be applied any time we are referencing the "who" of what we want to study. Speaking of the "who . . ." One final warning is that we know that there is a nuance to each character and how they are portrayed on television or in cartoons or in movies or in comics or in books or by the actors who portray them or by the directors who shape the various universes. We have struggled more than a bit with this. For example, if I say Batman's Robin, who do you think of? Dick Grayson? Jason Todd? Tim Drake? Carrie Kelley? Damian Wayne? If you ask any of the three of us, you might get a different answer, so if you ask us each how much we like Robin??? Well . . . it depends on which version you are asking about. In some cases, we spell this out for our characters (as you will see on this list), and sometimes we leave that up to how the participant defines the character. Is this a perfect solution? No, it is not; but it is a fun one that has led to some pretty great conversations at conventions.

Sample Items:

- Yoda (*Star Wars*)
- Darth Vader (*Star Wars*)
- Luke Skywalker (*Star Wars*)
- Old Ben Kenobi (Episode IV) (S*tar Wars*)
- Emperor Palpatine (*Star Wars*)
- Han Solo (Episodes IV, V, VI) (*Star Wars*)
- Princess Leia Organa (Episodes IV, V, VI) (S*tar Wars*)
- Kylo Ren (*Star Wars*)
- Rey (*Star Wars*)
- Finn (*Star Wars*)
- Boba Fett (*Star Wars*)
- Lando Calrissian (*Star Wars*)
- Jar Jar Binks (*Star Wars*)
- Senator Palpatine (Star Wars)
- General Obi-Wan Kenobi (Episodes I, II, III) (*Star Wars*)
- Queen Amidala/Padmé (*Star Wars*)
- General Grievous (*Star Wars*)
- Mace Windu (*Star Wars*)
- Jyn Erso (*Star Wars*)

- Eren/Mikasa (*Attack on Titan*)
- Levi/Eren (*Attack on Titan*)
- Levi/Erwin (*Attack on Titan*)
- Jean/Marco (*Attack on Titan*)
- Spike/Buffy (Spuffy) (*Buffy the Vampire Slayer*)
- Buffy/Angel (Bangel) (*Buffy the Vampire Slayer*)
- Aquaman/Mera (DC)
- Superman/Batman (DC)
- Superman/Wonder Woman (DC)
- Superman/Lois Lane (DC)
- Mickey/Minnie (Disney)
- Donald/Daisy (Disney)
- Anna/Kristoff (*Frozen*)
- Jack Skellington/Sally (*Nightmare Before Christmas*)
- Jack/Ianto (*Torchwood*)
- Jack/Rose (*Doctor Who*)
- Fry/Leela (*Futurama*)
- Cersei/Jaime (Lannicest) (*Game of Thrones*)
- Daenerys/Jon (Snowstorm) (*Game of Thrones*)
- Kurt/Blaine (Klaine) (*Glee*)
- Hamilton/Laurens (Lams) (*Hamilton*)
- Harry Potter/Hermione Granger (*Harry Potter*)
- Hermione Granger/Draco Malfoy (*Harry Potter*)
- Dumbledore/Grindelwald (*Harry Potter*)
- Captain America/Iron Man (Stony) (Marvel)
- Captain America/Winter Soldier (Stucky) (Marvel)
- Hellboy (Dark Horse)
- Crimson King (Dark Tower)
- Eddie Dean (Dark Tower)
- Beast Boy (DC)
- Black Adam (DC)
- Black Canary (DC)
- Steve Trevor (DC)
- Shazam (DC)
- Lucifer (*Lucifer* TV Show) (DC)
- Crazy Jane (*Doom Patrol*) (DC)
- Hoban "Wash" Washburne (*Firefly*)
- Jayne Cobb (*Firefly*)
- Mr. Wednesday Odin (Gaiman/*American Gods*)
- Shadow Moon (Gaiman/*American Gods*)
- Jaime Lannister (*Game of Thrones*)

- Joffrey Baratheon (*Game of Thrones*)
- Howl (Studio Ghibli)
- Jiji (Studio Ghibli)
- Kiki (Studio Ghibli)
- Totoro (Studio Ghibli)
- Aaron Burr (*Hamilton*)
- Dobby (*Harry Potter*)
- Dolores Umbridge (*Harry Potter*)
- Liv Moore (*iZombie*)
- John Wick (*John Wick*)
- David Haller (*Legion*)
- Aragorn (*Lord of the Rings*)
- Bilbo Baggins (*Lord of the Rings*)
- Frodo Baggins (*Lord of the Rings*)
- Gandalf (*Lord of the Rings*)
- Baron Zemo (Marvel)
- Beast/Hank McCoy (Marvel)
- Black Panther (Marvel)
- Black Widow (Marvel)
- Spider Gwen/Gwen Stacy (Marvel)
- Spider-Man/Peter Parker (Marvel)
- Spider-Man/Miles Morales (Marvel)
- Star Lord (Marvel)
- Magnus Bane (*Mortal Instruments*)
- Jonathan "Black Jack" Randall (*Outlander*)
- Archie (*Riverdale*)
- James T. Kirk (*Star Trek*)
- Kahn (*Star Trek*)
- Leonard McCoy/Bones (*Star Trek*)
- Amethyst (*Steven Universe*)
- Garnet (*Steven Universe*)
- Pearl (*Steven Universe*)
- Steven Universe (*Steven Universe*)
- Barbara Holland (*Stranger Things*)
- Chief Hopper (*Stranger Things*)
- Crowley (*Supernatural*)
- Dean Winchester (*Supernatural*)
- Sam Winchester (*Supernatural*)
- Edward Cullen (*Twilight*)
- Jacob Black (*Twilight*)
- Carl Grimes (*The Walking Dead*)

- Clementine Pennyfeather (*Westworld*)
- Dolores Abernathy (*Westworld*)
- Dr. Robert Ford (*Westworld*)
- Mulder (*X-Files*)
- Scully (*X-Files*)
- Vanya Hargreeves/Number Seven (*Umbrella Academy*)
- Luther Hargreeves/Number One (*Umbrella Academy*)
- Diego Hargreeves/Number Two (*Umbrella Academy*)
- Allison Hargreeves/Number Three (*Umbrella Academy*)
- Klaus Hargreeves/Number Four (*Umbrella Academy*)
- Crowley (Gaiman/*Good Omens*)
- Aziraphale (Gaiman/*Good Omens*)
- Sabrina Spellman (*Chilling Adventures of Sabrina*)
- Snoopy (*Peanuts*)
- Woodstock (*Peanuts*)
- Duke (*G.I. Joe*)
- Hawk (*G.I. Joe*)
- Kim Possible (*Kim Possible*)
- Ron Stoppable (*Kim Possible*)
- Scrooge McDuck (*DuckTales*)
- Huey Duck (*DuckTales*)
- Dewey Duck (*DuckTales*)
- Louie Duck (*DuckTales*)
- Rowlf the Dog (*Muppet Babies*)
- Gonzo (*Muppet Babies*)
- Winnie the Pooh (*New Adventure of Winnie the Pooh*)
- Tigger (*New Adventure of Winnie the Pooh*)
- He-Man/Prince Adam (*Masters of the Universe*)
- She-Ra/Princess Adora (*Masters of the Universe*)
- Porkchop (*Doug*)
- Quailman (*Doug*)
- Judith "Judy" Funnie (*Doug*)
- Arnold Phillip Shortman (*Hey Arnold*)
- Ren Höek (*The Ren & Stimpy Show*)
- Stimpson "Stimpy" J. Cat (*The Ren & Stimpy Show*)
- Tommy Pickles (*Rugrats*)
- Chuckie Finster (*Rugrats*)
- Phil DeVille (*Rugrats*)
- Lil DeVille (*Rugrats*)
- SpongeBob SquarePants (*SpongeBob SquarePants*)
- Patrick Star (*SpongeBob SquarePants*)

- Squidward Tentacles (*SpongeBob SquarePants*)
- Mr. Krabs (*SpongeBob SquarePants*)
- Timmy Turner (*Fairly Odd Parents*)
- Wanda (*Fairly Odd Parents*)
- Cosmo (*Fairly Odd Parents*)
- Leonardo (*Teenage Mutant Ninja Turtles*)
- Michelangelo (*Teenage Mutant Ninja Turtles*)
- Donatello (*Teenage Mutant Ninja Turtles*)
- Raphael (*Teenage Mutant Ninja Turtles*)
- Speed Racer (*The New Adventures of Speed Racer*)
- Inspector Gadget (*Inspector Gadget*)
- Brain (*Inspector Gadget*)
- Blossom (*Powerpuff Girls*)
- Buttercup (*Powerpuff Girls*)
- Bubbles (*Powerpuff Girls*)
- Professor (*Powerpuff Girls*)
- MoJo JoJo (*Powerpuff Girls*)
- Ed (*Ed, Edd n Eddy*)
- Edd (*Ed, Edd n Eddy*)
- Eddy (*Ed, Edd n Eddy*)
- Samurai Jack (*Samurai Jack*)
- Fred Flintstone (*The Flintstones*)
- Wilma Flintstone (*The Flintstones*)
- Scooby-Doo (*Scooby-Doo Where Are You?*)
- Bugs Bunny (*Looney Tunes*)
- Daffy Duck (*Looney Tunes*)
- Robin (*Teen Titans*)
- David Rose/Patrick Brewer (*Schitt's Creek*)
- Launchpad McQuack (*DuckTales*)
- Bucky Barnes/Winter Soldier (Marvel)
- Kermit the Frog (*Muppet Babies*)
- Piglet (*The New Adventures of Winnie the Pooh*)
- Max Goof (*Goof Troop*)
- Ickis (*Aaah!!! Real Monsters*)
- Patricia "Patti" Mayonnaise (*Doug*)
- Zim (*Invader Zim*)
- Baloo (*Talespin*)
- Grumpy Bear (*Care Bears*)
- Cheer Bear (*Care Bears*)
- Fry (*Futurama*)
- Bender (*Futurama*)

- Hank Hill (*King of the Hill*)
- Optimus Prime (*Transformers*)
- Kate Bishop/Hawkeye (Marvel)
- Katie
- *Paranormal Activity*
- Toby
- The Blair Witch
- Freddy Krueger
- *A Nightmare on Elm Street*
- *Freddy vs. Jason*
- Jason Voorhees
- *Friday the 13th*
- George Lutz
- *The Amityville Horror*
- Kathy Lutz
- Laurie Strode
- *Halloween*
- Michael Myers
- Damien Thorn
- *The Omen*
- Danny Torrance
- *The Shining*
- Norman Bates
- Lorraine Warren
- Ed Warren
- *Gremlins*
- *Krampus*
- *Annabelle*
- *Saw*
- Emily Rose
- *Cujo*
- *Carrie*
- *Salem's Lot*
- *The Stand*
- Captain Trips
- Arya Stark (*Game of Thrones*)
- Jon Snow (*Game of Thrones*)
- Theon Greyjoy (*Game of Thrones*)
- Cersei Lannister (*Game of Thrones*)
- Ghost (*Game of Thrones*)
- Sansa Stark (*Game of Thrones*)

- Gendry (*Game of Thrones*)
- Hodor (*Game of Thrones*)
- Jorah Mormont (*Game of Thrones*)
- Joffrey Baratheon (*Game of Thrones*)
- Khal Drogo (*Game of Thrones*)
- Ned Stark (*Game of Thrones*)
- Missandei (*Game of Thrones*)
- Night King (*Game of Thrones*)
- Lord "Littlefinger" Baelish (*Game of Thrones*)
- Robb Stark (*Game of Thrones*)
- Ramsay Bolton (*Game of Thrones*)
- Tormund (*Game of Thrones*)
- Ygritte (*Game of Thrones*)

Appendix C

Sample YouTubers (Internet Personalities) and Celebrities

Same as with the other appendixes, this is in no way an exhaustive list from the last decade of research. Remember, this is a composite list and not a comprehensive list. It only applies to chapters 6 and 7 in this book, but like fandoms (chapter 9) with lots of datasets collected and being analyzed in our upcoming studies. We set out to create something different in many ways with this list. We spent years combing through comic books, movies, cartoons, and television to create character lists to examine. In the process, we also got sucked into websites like Twitter, Tumblr, and even YouTube as we looked at how fans responded to characters and creators.

It also left some of us (mainly Britani) more than a little obsessed with YouTubers. That year, she had given up cable and made the move to solely streaming services and Internet-based entertainment. Much like many people, rather than leaving mindless reruns on in the background of daily life, YouTube became the background noise for dinners. It also highlighted just how similar YouTube content was to a lot of the things we had been studying. It had a large fan base and lots of "characters" to look at.

We developed this list by looking through previous VidCon (YouTube's large yearly fan convention) panel programming, articles that discussed content creators with high subscriber count (for the time of this study), and sources that discussed the evolution of YouTube's popularity. It is, again, by no means an exhaustive list or at this time a current list. YouTubers create many channels, and anyone can create a channel. Some become overnight successes, skyrocket to fame, and even flicker out. We tried to create a list that included a large variety of content creators and genres, just as we did with any of our previous studies.

While researching this list, which you will see in just a moment, we also started to see differences across various mediums and media in how people were treated, namely, how men and women were perceived when they found themselves airing their personal matters or struggles to the public. YouTube is somewhere people can pour out their stories to the camera and discuss their struggles. While looking at news and updates, we also found ourselves delving into stories about Demi Lovato and Mac Miller. Their stories of addiction and struggles. They felt connected. The Internet made them connected. All of this highlighted how much the Internet impacts views. Everything lives on the Internet. Robert Downey Jr., now famous for his movies and his acting, still has photos from his days of substance use, rehab, and jail, "living" on the Internet. Even when the creators themselves take down photos or videos they continue to live on in the worlds of the Internet thanks to trolls and technology.

The creators, artists, and individuals listed below represent just that: People who "live" on the Internet in one form or another. They have either found themselves famous thanks to YouTube, or their stories have been infamously blasted across the likes of Twitter and Buzzfeed News. As with our other projects, there was much discussion around who to include and how to create as diverse a list as possible. Now, it is easy to say that some of these names are not the most subscribed to on YouTube . . . which is why we are always adjusting, tweaking, and debating additions and subtractions to our lists. This, dear readers, is how we continue to find ourselves with 500 characters on any given list for every single project. It's always a work in progress as the pop culture zeitgeist waxes and wanes. It reflects us in the list maybe a bit too.

Sample Items:

- Demi Lovato
- Mac Miller
- Robert Downey Jr.
- Ariana Grande
- Lindsay Lohan
- Charlie Sheen
- Whitney Houston
- Amanda Bynes
- Britney Spears
- Prince
- Heath Ledger
- Kurt Cobain
- Courtney Love
- Robin Williams
- Kelly Osbourne
- Drew Barrymore

- Zac Efron
- Colin Farrell
- Russell Brand
- Katy Perry
- Dax Sheppard
- Ed Sheeran
- Matthew Perry
- Nicole Richie
- Eminem
- Philip Seymour Hoffman
- Corey Feldman
- Carrie Fisher
- Cory Monteith
- Lea Michelle
- Tatum O'Neal
- Keith Richards
- Michael Phelps
- Amy Winehouse
- Johnny Depp
- David Cassidy
- Justin Bieber
- Ben Affleck
- Jennifer Garner
- Jamie Lee Curtis
- Keith Urban
- Nicole Kidman
- Michael Jackson
- Wilmer Valderrama
- Miley Cyrus
- Liam Hemsworth
- Bobby Brown
- Chris Farley
- Pete Davidson
- Jimi Hendrix
- Janis Joplin
- Marilyn Monroe
- Tom Petty
- River Phoenix
- Elvis Presley
- Anna Nicole Smith
- G-Eazy

- Halsey
- John Belushi
- Jim Morrison
- Judy Garland
- Amy Poehler
- Anthony Bourdain
- Asia Argento
- Ozzy Osbourne
- Sharon Osbourne
- Mel Gibson
- Rihanna
- Snoop Lion
- Corey Haim
- DJ AM
- Sid Vicious
- Nancy Spungen
- Kirsten Dunst
- Edie Falco
- Kristen Bell
- Daniel Middleton (DanTDM)
- David Dobrik
- Ethan and Grayson Dolan (Dolan Twins)
- Dude Perfect
- Seán McLoughlin (jacksepticeye)
- Arin and Dan (GameGrumps)
- Olajide Olatunji (KSI)
- Liza Koshy
- Patrick Starrr
- Safiya Nygaard
- James Charles
- Jeffree Star (JeffreeStar)
- TheOdd1sOut
- Dodie Clark (DoodleOddle)
- Elle Mills (ElleoftheMills)
- Eric Ochoa (SUPEReeeGo)
- Anna Akana
- Miranda Sings
- Phillip DeFranco
- Ian Carter (iDubbbz)
- Bryan Le (RiceGum)
- Mark Fischbach (Markiplier)

- Grace Helbig
- Joey Graceffa
- MyLifeAsEva
- Hannah Hart and Ella Mielniczenko (MyHarto)
- Hank and John Green (Vlogbrothers)
- De'Arra and Ken (DK4L)
- Gigi Gorgeous
- Jenn Mcallister (Jennxpenn)
- Casey Neistat
- Rosanna Pansino (Nerdy Nummies)
- Matthew Patrick (MatPat) Game Theory; Film Theory)
- Lauren Riihimaki (LaurDIY)
- Christine Sydelko
- Brandon Rogers
- Veronica Jo and Vanessa Jo Merrell (MerrellTwins)
- Alex Wassabi (Wassabi)
- Aaron Kyro (Braille Skateboarding)
- Burnie Burns (Rooster Teeth)
- Geoff Ramsey (Rooster Teeth; Achievement Hunter)
- Adelaine Morin
- Alexis G. Zall
- Alexys Fleming (MadeYewLook)
- AlishaMarie
- Andrea Russett
- Andrea's Choice
- Andrew Huang
- Andrew Rea (Binging with Babish)
- Anna Brisbin (BrizzyVoices)
- Anthony Padilla
- Aphmau
- Ashley Perez (Buzzfeed)
- BeautyByNena (NENA)
- Benny and Rafi Fine (Fine Brothers; React)
- Boogie2988
- Brandon Laatsch (BrandonJLa)
- Chachi Gonzales
- Chantel Houston (Buzzfeed)
- Rob Czar and Corinne Leigh (Threadbanger)
- Coyote Peterson (Brave Wilderness)
- Cristine (Simply Nailogical)
- Bryan and Missy (Daily Bumps)

- DangMattSmith
- Destin Sandlin (Smarter Every Day)
- Devin Lytle
- Dianna Cowern (Physics Girl)
- Domics
- Domo and Crissy
- Dormtainment
- Adam Conover (Adam Ruins Everything)
- Draw with Jazza
- Alex Clark (ItsAlexClark)
- Dulce Candy
- Dytto
- Elijah Daniel
- Emma Blackery
- Essence Gant (Buzzfeed)
- Evan, Michael, and Andrew Gregory (Schmoyoho; The Gregory Brothers)
- Freddie Wong (Rocket Jump)
- SungWon Cho (ProZD)
- Gabbie Hanna
- ItsBambi
- Jack Douglass (JacksFilms)
- JaidenAnimations
- Michael Stevens (VSauce3)
- JC Caylen
- Jenn Im
- JoJo Siwa (ItsJoJoSiwa)
- Joe Hanson (It's Okay To Be Smart)
- Joe Cozart (Paint)
- Jordan Maron (CaptainSparklez)
- Jordyn Jones
- Justine Ezarik (iJustine)
- Kandee Johnson
- Karina Garcia
- KellieSweet
- Kevin LaSean (XPertThief)
- Kingsley
- Kristin Chirico (Buzzfeed; Ladylike)
- Kristine and Matt (Family Fun Pack)
- Kyle Hanagami
- LDShadowLady
- LaToya Forever

- Laura Lee
- LaurenzSide
- Leroy Sanchez
- Luke Korns
- MacDoesIt
- Madilyn Bailey
- Mamrie Hart
- Manny Mua
- Matt Steffanina
- Marshmello
- Meg DeAngelis (MayBaby)
- Megan Nicole (MeganNicoleMusic)
- Mia Stammer (MamaMiaMakeup)
- Mikey Murphy
- Miles McKenna (MilesChronicles)
- MissRemiAshten
- Molly Burke
- Natalie Alzate (NataliesOutlet)
- Niana Guerrero
- Nikita Dragun
- Olivia Jade
- Peter Hollens
- Pokimane
- Rachel Ballinger
- Rachel Levin (Rclbeauty101)
- Ranz Kyle
- Rebecca Zamolo
- Ricky Dillon
- Rob Scallion
- Roi Fabito (Guava Juice)
- Roomie
- Sandi Ball (CutePolish; CutePlay)
- Sean Evans (Hot Ones)
- Sierra Furtado
- SmallishBeans
- StacyPlays
- Steven Lim, Andrew Ilnyckyj, and Adam Bianchi (Buzzfeed Worth It)
- Dave Brown (BoyInABand)
- Strawburry17
- Teala Dunn (TTLYTEALA)
- Tessa Violet

- Katie and Billy (The Bratayleys)
- Thomas Sanders
- Tiffany Herrera (IHasCupquake; TiffyQuake)
- Tina Yong (TinaCreative)
- Yolanda Gampp (How To Cake It)
- Trevor Moran
- Tré Melvin
- Zach King
- Bill Wurtz
- Adande Thorne (Swoozie)
- Bella Thorn
- Tana Mongeau
- Shane Dawson
- Eugene Lee Yang (Try Guys)
- Keith Habersberger (Try Guys)
- Ned Fulmer (Try Guys)
- Zach Kornfeld (Try Guys)
- H2O Delirious
- Luke Patterson (CartoonZ)
- Evan Fong (VanossGaming)
- Ethan and Hila Klein (H3H3 Productions)
- Caspar Lee
- Harley Morenstein (Epic Meal Time)
- Jenna Mourey (Jenna Marbles)
- Julien Solomita
- Ladylike
- Clevver
- Wisecrack
- Smosh
- Lachlan
- LazarBeam
- Lilly Singh (IISuperwomanII)
- Jake Paul
- Logan Paul
- Muselk
- Ryan Higa (Nigahiga)
- Ninja
- Felix Kjellberg (PewDiePie)
- Reaction Time
- Rhett and Link (Good Mythical Morning)
- Shane and Ryan (Buzzfeed Unsolved)

- SSSniperWolf
- Trisha Paytas
- Tyler Oakley
- David Dobrik
- BadLipReading
- Kevin O'Reilly (CallMeKevin)
- Garnt (Gigguk)
- GradeAUnderA
- Jeremy Jahns
- Primitive Technology
- SuperMarioLogan
- TeamFourStar
- Jason Gastrow (VideoGameDunkey)
- You Suck At Cooking
- Triggered Tro

Appendix D
Sample Fandoms

Once again, this is in no way an exhaustive list from the last decade of research. Considering that we created our first list in the early days of our research by arguing for our own favorite fandoms, it is pretty shocking to these authors that we really did not start looking at fandoms independently until a couple of years ago. We have measured fandoms in three ways. First, we added the fandom measure discussed in chapter 9. In addition to adding this measure to most of our new surveys and projects (really all of the studies that it is even remotely related to), we have also designed some of our lists specifically around fandoms. This allows us to get a deeper examination of a particular fandom rather than just the views of the fandom from the broader, more well-known, and popular characters and movies/shows. For example, we now have specific projects examining each of the following: *Star Wars*, *Supernatural*, Disney, Nickelodeon, YouTube Influencers, Cartoon Network, *Game of Thrones*, *Harry Potter*, and Christmas. In some of these cases, we are examining these fandoms in excruciating detail. Harry Potter, Disney, and YouTube have all been banes of our existence at one point. Britani once constructed a 200-plus item list, and we had some fantastically (see what we did there) cool results except for one small detail . . . she forgot to put Harry Potter on the list. We think everyone is aware of how April feels about Disney by now, and Keith only knows JoJo Siwa . . . and that's the only YouTuber he knows because we tricked him into wearing a JoJo bow for a con panel.

Secondly, we have started asking individuals to specifically identify their favorite fandoms. This is, maybe, the hardest question that we ask participants. We know that settling on a single fandom is next to impossible. In fact, we think any of the three of us would be hard pressed to identify a single fandom. Even Keith, with his mighty love for both Superman and Mickey Mouse, would have difficulty choosing just one fandom. Poor Britani is a member of pretty much any fandom that she encounters. April has more discerning tastes (she is one of those weird humans who gets bored 15 minutes into a show or movie and will just literally walk away), but if you made her choose, the best you could hope for would be "horror." In fact, we created some very broad categories of fandoms just because of this. We still make people pick. It gives us one more piece of convergent (or divergent) evidence. Remember, this is a composite list and not a comprehensive list. It only applies to chapter 9 in this book, but with lots of datasets to come (we are currently collecting data on about six studies, as of the writing of this book).

Sample Items:

- Choose which fandom you most associate as being a member of
    - *Marvel Universe* (TV and Cinematic Universe)
    - *Star Wars* (all nine Episodes, spin-offs, and cartoons)
    - *Star Trek* (original and reboot)
    - *My Little Pony* (original and the reboot)
    - *Pokémon*
    - *DC Universe* (DC TV, Cinematic Universe, and comics/graphic novels)
    - *Harry Potter* (and the Harry Potter Universe)
    - *Lord of the Rings* (LOTR and The Hobbit)
    - *The Walking Dead* (TV and comics/graphic novels)
    - *Game of Thrones*
    - *Supernatural*
    - *Doctor Who*
    - Fortnite
    - Minecraft
    - Anime (we know this is a broad topic, but in addition to breaking these out into examples, we have also treated it like Disney and created a larger subcategory that includes all things anime)
    - *Sherlock*
    - *Percy Jackson*
    - *Attack on Titan*
    - *Steven Universe*
    - *Buffy the Vampire Slayer*
    - *The Vampire Diaries*
    - *Rick and Morty*
    - Disney
    - *Good Omens*
    - *Voltron*

- Horror (this is another category that is massively too broad, but April has had MUCH difficulty getting Keith and Britani to watch anything scary or gory because they are wimps like that—feel free to find them on social media and peer pressure them into some of the classics that they are TOTALLY missing)
- *My Hero Academia*
- *Firefly*
- Arrowverse
- YouTube
- *The Office*
- *Friends*
- *Gilmore Girls*
- *Stranger Things*
- *Grey's Anatomy*
- I'm not really into fandoms (yes, this is a thing, and we do give participants this option—but we will admit that we feel sorry for those humans)

Index

About the Authors

Keith W. Beard, Psy.D., has a master's degree in clinical psychology, and his Psy.D. degree is in clinical psychology. Beyond his academic work, he has worked in university counseling centers, community mental health centers, and currently has a small private practice. His interests are primarily in abnormal psychology, personality, sexuality studies, and Internet addiction. Dr. Beard has also taught a wide array of courses (Introductory Psychology, Paranormal Phenomena, Abnormal Psychology, Personality, Group Therapy, Psychotherapy, and Human Sexuality) and incorporates those into our projects.

April Fugett, Ph.D., has a master's degree is a general psychology, and a Ph.D. in cognitive psychology. Her primary interests are in language, memory, research methodology, and statistical analyses. She has taught a wide array of courses for each program in her Department, from Introduction to Psychology for Freshmen, to Psychology of the Apocalypse for Juniors and Seniors, to Advanced Quantitative Analysis for fourth year doctoral students. She brings all these areas of expertise and experience into our research.

Britani Black, Psy.D., has a master's degree in psychology and a Psy.D. in clinical psychology. She has also taught a wide array of courses, including Internet Famous: Language, Health, and Psychology in the Age of the New Celebrity and The Heroes and Villains of Healthcare, and has clinical expertise in interpersonal theories, substance use, and young adult populations that she now uses to inform our projects.

CPSIA information can be obtained
at www.ICGtesting.com
Printed in the USA
LVHW040430290822
726885LV00004B/161